Crisp High Protein Air Fryer Power Meals Cookbook

Sculpt Your Diet with Flavorful Recipes With Photos

By Bella Bistro

Copyright © by Bella Bistro

This book is intended to provide helpful and informative material on high-protein cooking with an air fryer. The recipes and content within are designed to offer readers options for healthier, protein-rich meals that do not sacrifice flavor for nutritional value. The publisher and author do not assume any responsibility for errors, omissions, or damages resulting from using the information contained herein.

The recipes in this cookbook are original works created by the author and have been tested to ensure quality and accuracy. The accompanying photographs are also original, specifically taken to complement each recipe and assist readers in achieving similar results.

"Crisp High Protein Air Fryer Power Meals Cookbook" and "Sculpt Your Diet with Flavorful Recipes With Photos" are trademarks of Bella Bistro Publishing. Unauthorized use of these trademarks without the express written consent of Bella Bistro Publishing is strictly prohibited.

The author and publisher have made every effort to ensure that this book's cooking instructions and ingredients are accurate and effective. However, readers are advised to adjust their cooking methods and ingredient choices to suit personal dietary needs and equipment specifications.

Thank you for respecting the hard work of this author. Enjoy your culinary journey with "Crisp High Protein Air Fryer Power Meals Cookbook," where high protein meets high flavor.

Introduction

Are you looking to boost your protein intake without sacrificing flavor or convenience? Look no further! Bella Bistro's "Crisp High Protein Air Fryer Power Meals Cookbook" delivers 50 high-protein recipes that are as nourishing as they are delightful, all tailored for your air fryer.

This cookbook bridges the gap between health and taste, offering various meals that cater to all preferences and meal times. Organized into five chapters: Chicken, Meat, Fish & Seafood, Vegetables, and Snacks. Each section includes 10 innovative recipes designed to maximize nutritional value and ease of cooking.

Here's what makes this cookbook a must-have in your kitchen:

- **50 Authentic Recipes:** Explore a world of robust flavors with recipes crafted for taste and health, ensuring you receive the protein your body needs in every bite.

- **Vibrant, Original Photos:** Each recipe comes with a stunning, full-color photo that inspires you and guides you to achieving the perfect dish.

- **Easy-to-Follow Instructions:** No matter your cooking skill level, the instructions are straightforward and simple, allowing you to replicate dishes to perfection.

- **High-Quality Print:** The standard color printed paperback is practical and aesthetically pleasing, making it a delightful addition to your collection.

- **Perfectly Tested Flavors:** Each recipe has been rigorously tested to ensure it meets the highest standards of taste and texture.

- **Impeccable Quality:** This book has been carefully edited to ensure it is free from grammatical or spelling errors, allowing for a smooth, enjoyable cooking experience.

Take advantage of the opportunity to transform your meals into power-packed, delicious experiences. Today, grab your copy of "Crisp High Protein Air Fryer Power Meals Cookbook" and start sculpting your diet with every crispy, protein-rich meal. Dive into the delicious convenience of air frying and enjoy the benefits of a high-protein diet without the hassle.

Table of Contents

Chapter 01: Protein-Packed Chicken

← ─────────────────────────────────────── →

Recipe 01: Whole Roasted Chicken

Dive into the world of healthy, protein-packed meals with this Whole Roasted Chicken With Garnish recipe, perfectly crafted for your air fryer. Effortless yet exquisite, it promises a delightful dinner to your table.

Servings: 4

Cook Time: 60 mins

Prepping Time: 15 mins

Difficulty: Easy

Ingredients:

- ✓ 1 whole chicken (about 4 lbs)
- ✓ 2 tbsp olive oil
- ✓ 1 tsp salt
- ✓ 1/2 tsp black pepper
- ✓ 1 tsp garlic powder
- ✓ 1 tsp dried thyme
- ✓ 1 lemon, halved
- ✓ 4 garlic cloves
- ✓ Fresh herbs for garnish (rosemary, thyme, parsley)

Step-by-Step Preparation:

1. Preheat your air fryer to 360°F.
2. Rinse the chicken and pat dry with paper towels.
3. Rub the chicken evenly with olive oil, then season with salt, pepper, garlic powder, and thyme.
4. Stuff the cavity with lemon halves and garlic cloves.
5. Place the chicken in the air fryer basket, breast side down, and cook for 30 minutes. Flip and cook for 30 minutes or until golden and cooked through.
6. Let the chicken rest for 10 minutes before garnishing with fresh herbs.

Nutritional Facts: (Per serving)

- ❖ Calories: 520
- ❖ Protein: 43g
- ❖ Fat: 36g
- ❖ Carbohydrates: 2g
- ❖ Sodium: 620mg

Embark on a culinary journey that marries simplicity with elegance. This Whole Roasted Chicken recipe, tailored for your air fryer, guarantees a juicy, flavorful feast bound to impress. High in protein and low in carbs, it's the perfect centerpiece for a nutritious family dinner.

Recipe 02: Skinless Chicken Breast With Spices

Elevate your dinner game with this high-protein, skinless chicken breast recipe, masterfully seasoned and air-fried to perfection. Quick, healthy, and irresistibly flavorful, this dish is a testament to the simplicity and joy of cooking at home.

Servings: 2

Prepping Time: 10 mins

Cook Time: 20 mins

Difficulty: Medium

Ingredients:

- ✓ 2 skinless chicken breasts
- ✓ 1 tbsp olive oil
- ✓ 1 tsp paprika
- ✓ 1 tsp garlic powder
- ✓ 1/2 tsp ground cumin
- ✓ 1/2 tsp salt
- ✓ 1/4 tsp black pepper
- ✓ 1/2 tsp dried oregano
- ✓ 1/4 tsp chili powder (optional for a spicy kick)

Step-by-Step Preparation:

1. Preheat the air fryer to 375°F.
2. In a small bowl, mix the olive oil with all the spices.
3. Brush the spice mixture onto both sides of the chicken breasts, ensuring they are well coated.
4. Place the chicken breasts in the air fryer basket, ensuring they're not touching for even cooking.
5. Cook 10 minutes, flip, and cook for 10 minutes or until the internal temperature reaches 165°F.
6. Remove the chicken from the air fryer and let it rest for a few minutes before serving.

Nutritional Facts: (Per serving)

- ❖ Calories: 230
- ❖ Protein: 26g
- ❖ Fat: 13g
- ❖ Carbohydrates: 1g
- ❖ Sodium: 400mg

Discover the essence of healthy and delicious cooking with this skinless chicken breast recipe, a perfect blend of spices and tenderness made in an air fryer. Whether you want to impress guests or indulge in a nutritious meal, this dish promises satisfaction with every bite.

Recipe 03: Drummet Chicken With Fish Sauce

Savor the umami-rich flavors of Air Fryer Drumstick Chicken with Fish Sauce, a high-protein dish that combines succulence and zest in every bite. This recipe offers a novel twist on classic chicken drumsticks, promising a culinary adventure from your kitchen.

Servings: 4

Prepping Time: 15 mins

Cook Time: 25 mins

Difficulty: Easy

Ingredients:

- ✓ 8 chicken drumsticks
- ✓ 2 tbsp fish sauce
- ✓ 1 tbsp soy sauce
- ✓ 2 tbsp brown sugar
- ✓ 3 cloves garlic, minced
- ✓ 1 tbsp ginger, grated
- ✓ 1 tbsp lime juice
- ✓ 1/2 tsp black pepper
- ✓ 1 tbsp olive oil
- ✓ Fresh cilantro for garnish
- ✓ Sliced lime wedges for serving

Step-by-Step Preparation:

1. Whisk together fish sauce, soy sauce, brown sugar, garlic, ginger, lime juice, and black pepper in a bowl to create the marinade.
2. Coat the drumsticks evenly with the marinade and let them sit in the refrigerator for at least 1 hour.
3. Preheat the air fryer to 380°F.
4. Brush the air fryer basket with olive oil and place the marinated drumsticks in the basket.
5. Cook for 25 minutes, turning halfway through, until the chicken is golden and fully cooked.
6. Garnish with fresh cilantro and serve with lime wedges on the side.

Nutritional Facts: (Per serving)

- ❖ Calories: 310
- ❖ Protein: 27g
- ❖ Fat: 18g
- ❖ Carbohydrates: 8g
- ❖ Sodium: 900mg

Experience the delightful blend of flavors with Air Fryer Drumstick Chicken with Fish Sauce, where the savory essence of fish sauce meets the tenderness of chicken in a dance of taste and texture. Ideal for any day of the week, this dish brings a touch of gourmet to your everyday meals, ensuring a dining experience that's both nutritious and indulgent.

Recipe 04: Chicken Wings Glazed With Hot Chili Sauce

Unleash the fiery delight of Air Fryer Chicken Wings glazed with hot chili sauce, a high-protein feast that brings the heat to your table. Perfectly crispy, these wings are a game-changer for spice lovers, offering a blend of flavors that cater to all your sauce-dipping desires.

Servings: 4

Prepping Time: 10 mins

Cook Time: 24 mins

Difficulty: Medium

Ingredients:

- ✓ 2 lbs chicken wings, split at joints, tips removed
- ✓ 1 tbsp vegetable oil
- ✓ 1 tsp salt
- ✓ 1/2 tsp black pepper
- ✓ 1/2 cup hot chili sauce
- ✓ 1 tbsp honey
- ✓ 2 cloves garlic, minced
- ✓ Optional for serving: ranch dressing, blue cheese dressing, and celery sticks

Step-by-Step Preparation:

1. Toss chicken wings in a bowl with vegetable oil, salt, and pepper.
2. Preheat the air fryer to 380°F.
3. Arrange wings in the air fryer basket in a single layer; cook for 12 minutes. Flip the wings and cook for another 12 minutes until crispy.
4. While the wings are cooking, combine hot chili sauce, honey, and minced garlic in a saucepan over low heat. Simmer until the mixture is well combined.
5. Toss cooked wings in the chili sauce mixture.
6. Serve hot with dipping sauces and celery sticks on the side.

Nutritional Facts: (Per serving)

- ❖ Calories: 310
- ❖ Protein: 23g
- ❖ Fat: 22g
- ❖ Carbohydrates: 5g
- ❖ Sodium: 800mg

Dive into a world where heat meets meat, and every bite is a burst of flavor with these Air Fryer Chicken Wings glazed with hot chili sauce. Whether it's game day or a special treat, this dish will leave your taste buds dancing and craving more. Paired with an array of sauces, it's a culinary experience to be noticed.

Recipe 05: Chicken Roasted With Persimmon

Immerse yourself in the unique fusion of savory and sweet with this Tasty Chicken Meat roasted with Persimmon. A culinary delight that marries the juiciness of chicken breast with the luscious sweetness of Persimmon, creating a high-protein, flavorful dish that's as nutritious as it is delicious, all effortlessly prepared in your air fryer.

Servings: 4

Cook Time: 25 mins

Prepping Time: 15 mins

Difficulty: Easy

Ingredients:

- ✓ 4 chicken breasts
- ✓ 2 ripe persimmons, sliced
- ✓ 1 tbsp olive oil
- ✓ 1 tsp salt
- ✓ 1/2 tsp ground black pepper
- ✓ 1/2 tsp dried rosemary
- ✓ 1/2 tsp dried thyme
- ✓ 1 garlic clove, minced

Step-by-Step Preparation:

1. Preheat the air fryer to 360°F.

2. Rub each chicken breast with olive oil and then season with salt, pepper, rosemary, thyme, and garlic.

3. Arrange the chicken breasts in the air fryer basket and surround them with persimmon slices.

4. Cook for 25 minutes until the chicken is cooked and the persimmons tender.

5. Halfway through cooking, flip the chicken breasts and stir the persimmons to ensure even cooking.

Nutritional Facts: **(Per serving)**

- ❖ Calories: 210
- ❖ Protein: 31g
- ❖ Fat: 6g
- ❖ Carbohydrates: 10g
- ❖ Sodium: 630mg

This Tasty Chicken Meat roasted with Persimmon recipe promises a feast for the senses and a wholesome dining experience. Perfect for those seeking to explore the delightful harmony of fruit and poultry, it's a dish that brings a touch of gourmet to your everyday meals, all while keeping health at the forefront.

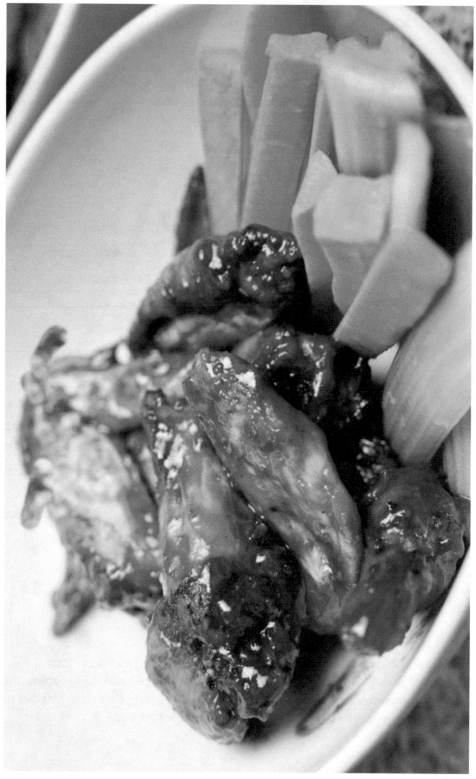

Recipe 06: Chicken Wings With Buffalo and Barbecue Sauce

Experience the ultimate comfort food with a twist in this Chicken Wings recipe, perfectly made in an air fryer. Combining the classic tang of buffalo sauce with the sweet and smoky depths of barbecue sauce, these wings promise an irresistibly delicious high-protein treat. Served with fresh carrots and celery sticks, it's a dish that balances indulgence with a touch of health.

Servings: 4

Prepping Time: 10 mins

Cook Time: 20 mins

Difficulty: Easy

Ingredients:

- ✓ 2 lbs chicken wings
- ✓ 1/2 cup buffalo sauce
- ✓ 1/2 cup barbecue sauce
- ✓ 1 tbsp olive oil
- ✓ Salt and pepper to taste
- ✓ Carrot sticks, for garnish
- ✓ Celery sticks for garnish
- ✓ Ranch or blue cheese dressing for dipping (optional)

Step-by-Step Preparation:

1. Preheat the air fryer to 400°F.
2. Toss the chicken wings with olive oil, salt, and pepper.
3. Arrange the wings in the air fryer basket and cook for 20 minutes, flipping halfway through until crispy.
4. In a large bowl, mix the buffalo sauce and barbecue sauce.
5. Toss the cooked wings in the sauce mixture until well coated.
6. Serve the wings garnished with carrot and celery sticks and ranch or blue cheese dressing if desired.

Nutritional Facts: (Per serving)

- ❖ Calories: 320
- ❖ Protein: 24g
- ❖ Fat: 22g
- ❖ Carbohydrates: 8g
- ❖ Sodium: 880mg

Elevate your game night, party, or dinner with these Chicken Wings made in an air fryer, a dish that's as easy to make as it is satisfying to eat. With the perfect balance of flavors and textures, along with the fresh crunch of carrot and celery sticks, this recipe offers a delightful way to enjoy your favorite comfort food.

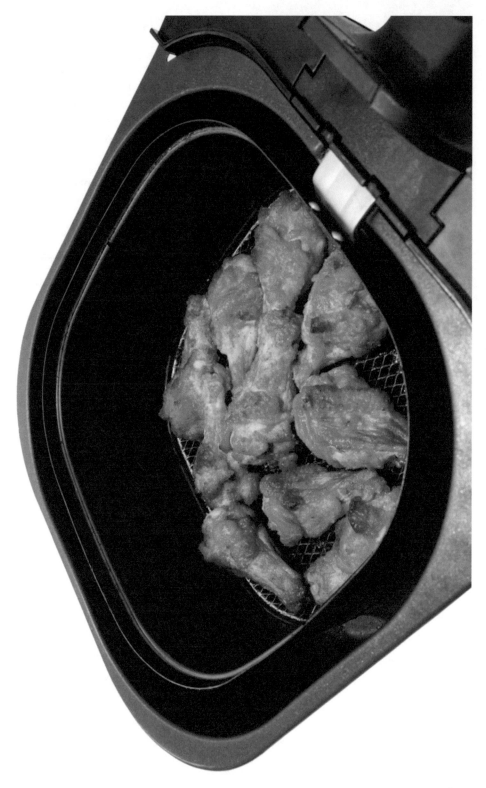

Recipe 07: Spices and Herbs Fermented Chicken Roasted

Embark on a culinary adventure with Spices and Herbs Fermented Chicken Roasted, a recipe that infuses high-protein chicken with fermentation's rich, complex flavors. Crafted for the air fryer, this dish brings a delightful twist to the traditional roast, combining ease with gourmet flair for a memorable dining experience.

Servings: 4

Prepping Time: 24 hours (for fermentation) + 15 mins

Cook Time: 45 mins

Difficulty: Intermediate

Ingredients:

- ✓ 4 chicken thighs (bone-in, skin-on)
- ✓ 1/4 cup homemade or store-bought fermented spice paste (garlic, onion, chili, and herbs)
- ✓ 1 tbsp olive oil
- ✓ 1 tsp sea salt
- ✓ 1/2 tsp ground black pepper
- ✓ Fresh herbs (rosemary, thyme) for garnish

Step-by-Step Preparation:

1. Rub the chicken thighs with the fermented spice paste. Cover and let them ferment in the refrigerator for 24 hours.
2. Preheat your air fryer to 380°F.
3. Lightly coat the chicken with olive oil and season with salt and pepper.
4. Place the chicken in the air fryer basket, skin-side up, and cook for 45 minutes or until the chicken is golden and the internal temperature reaches 165°F.
5. Garnish with fresh herbs before serving.

Nutritional Facts: (Per serving)

- ❖ Calories: 310
- ❖ Protein: 25g
- ❖ Fat: 22g
- ❖ Carbohydrates: 1g
- ❖ Sodium: 620mg

Discover the depth of flavor fermentation brings with this Spices and Herbs Fermented Chicken Roasted recipe. Perfect for those who appreciate the art of cooking with fermented ingredients, this dish offers a protein-packed, flavorful experience that's sure to impress. Enjoy the ease of air frying and the gourmet taste of slow-fermented spices.

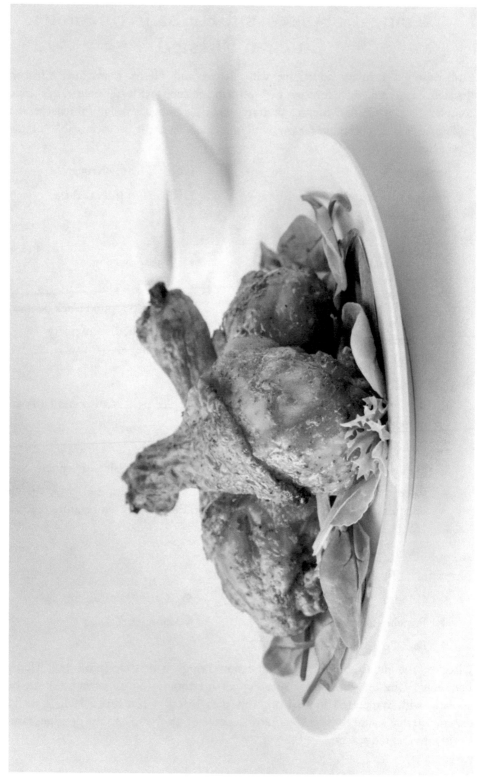

Recipe 08: Cooked Legs of Chicken With Spinach

Delight in the simple yet sophisticated taste of Cooked Legs of Chicken with Spinach, a high-protein, nutritious dish that perfectly combines juicy chicken with spinach's fresh, leafy greens. This recipe is prepared in an air fryer and offers a healthier, quicker alternative to traditional cooking methods without compromising flavor or quality.

Servings: 4   **Cook Time:** 30 mins

Prepping Time: 10 mins   **Difficulty:** Easy

Ingredients:

- ✔ 4 chicken legs
- ✔ 2 tbsp olive oil
- ✔ 1 tsp garlic powder
- ✔ 1 tsp smoked paprika
- ✔ Salt and pepper to taste
- ✔ 4 cups fresh spinach
- ✔ 1 tbsp lemon juice
- ✔ 1/2 tsp nutmeg

Step-by-Step Preparation:

1. Preheat the air fryer to 380°F.
2. Rub chicken legs with 1 tablespoon of olive oil, garlic powder, smoked paprika, salt, and pepper.
3. Place the chicken in the air fryer basket for 30 minutes or until crispy and cooked.
4. While the chicken is cooking, sauté spinach in the remaining olive oil over medium heat until wilted, about 2-3 minutes. Season with lemon juice, nutmeg, salt, and pepper.
5. Serve the chicken hot over a bed of seasoned spinach.

Nutritional Facts: (Per serving)

- ❖ Calories: 290
- ❖ Protein: 27g
- ❖ Fat: 18g
- ❖ Carbohydrates: 3g
- ❖ Sodium: 200mg

Savor the tender, flavorful chicken and nutrient-rich spinach in this Cooked Legs of Chicken with Spinach recipe. A feast for the senses, this dish is a testament to the beauty of simple ingredients coming together to create a satisfying and healthful meal. Perfect for a wholesome dinner, it's sure to become a staple in your cooking repertoire.

Recipe 09: Grilled Spicy Chicken Wings With Ketchup

Ignite your taste buds with Grilled Spicy Chicken Wings with Ketchup, a fiery twist on a beloved classic. This high-protein air fryer recipe delivers the perfect blend of heat and sweetness, guaranteeing to spice up your mealtime. Whether hosting a game day feast or looking for a quick and satisfying dinner, these wings promise to be a crowd-pleaser.

Servings: 4

Cook Time: 20 mins

Prepping Time: 15 mins

Difficulty: Easy

Ingredients:

- ✓ 2 lbs chicken wings
- ✓ 1 tbsp olive oil
- ✓ 1 tsp salt
- ✓ 1/2 tsp black pepper
- ✓ 2 tbsp hot sauce
- ✓ 1/4 cup ketchup
- ✓ 1 tbsp honey
- ✓ 1 tsp garlic powder
- ✓ 1 tsp smoked paprika

Step-by-Step Preparation:

1. Preheat the air fryer to 400°F.
2. Toss chicken wings with olive oil, salt, and pepper.
3. Cook in the air fryer for 20 minutes, flipping halfway through, until crispy.
4. While the wings cook, combine hot sauce, ketchup, honey, garlic powder, and smoked paprika in a bowl to make the glaze.
5. Once cooked, toss the wings in the glaze until evenly coated.
6. Serve immediately for the best flavor.

Nutritional Facts: (Per serving)

- ❖ Calories: 310
- ❖ Protein: 24g
- ❖ Fat: 22g
- ❖ Carbohydrates: 9g
- ❖ Sodium: 950mg

Embrace the heat with these Grilled Spicy Chicken Wings with Ketchup, a dish that brings the sizzle to your air fryer and the flavor to your plate. Simple, spicy, and utterly delicious, this recipe is a testament to the power of combining essential ingredients to create something extraordinary. Perfect for any occasion, it's sure to leave you craving more.

Recipe 10: Barbecue Chicken Wings and Drumsticks With Hot Chili Mango Sauce

Step into a world of flavor with Traditional Barbecue Chicken Wings and Drumsticks, elevated with an irresistible Hot Chili Mango Sauce and fresh coriander. This high-protein air fryer recipe melds the smoky essence of barbecue with the exotic sweetness of mango and the kick of chili, creating a dish that dances on the palate. It's a culinary celebration that brings a vibrant twist to classic favorites.

Servings: 4

Prepping Time: 20 mins

Cook Time: 25 mins

Difficulty: Medium

Ingredients:

- ✓ 2 lbs mix of chicken wings and drumsticks
- ✓ 1 tbsp olive oil
- ✓ Salt and pepper to taste
- ✓ 1/2 cup barbecue sauce
- ✓ 1 mango, pureed
- ✓ 1 tbsp hot chili sauce
- ✓ 1 tsp garlic, minced
- ✓ 1 lime, juiced
- ✓ Fresh coriander, chopped for garnish

Step-by-Step Preparation:

1. Preheat the air fryer to 400°F.
2. Toss chicken pieces with olive oil, salt, and pepper.
3. Cook in the air fryer for 25 minutes, turning halfway through, until crispy and golden.
4. While the chicken cooks, mix the barbecue sauce, mango puree, hot chili sauce, minced garlic, and lime juice in a bowl.
5. Once the chicken is done, toss it in the mango chili sauce until well coated.
6. Garnish with chopped coriander before serving.

Nutritional Facts: (Per serving)

- ❖ Calories: 325
- ❖ Protein: 22g
- ❖ Fat: 15g
- ❖ Carbohydrates: 22g
- ❖ Sodium: 650mg

Discover the perfect balance of sweet, spicy, and smoky in these Traditional Barbecue Chicken Wings and Drumsticks with Hot Chili Mango Sauce. This recipe brings an innovative twist to your dining table, ensuring each bite has flavor and freshness. Ideal for any gathering or a family dinner, it's a sure way to impress and satisfy.

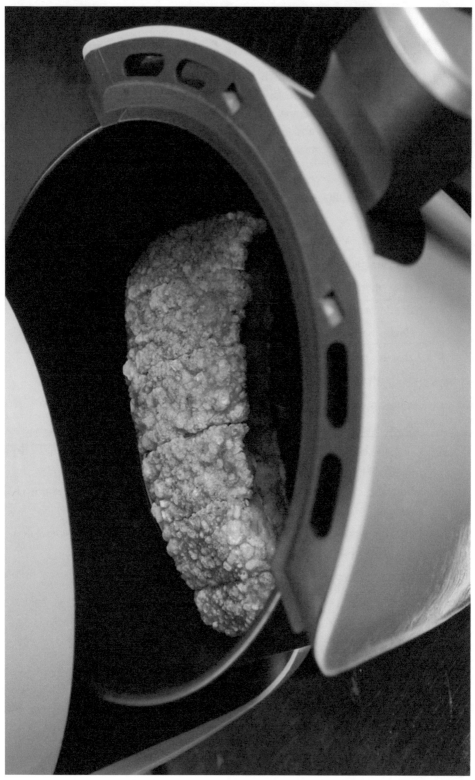

Chapter 02: Mighty Meat Dishes

Recipe 11: Crispy Pork With Air Fryers

Dive into a healthier lifestyle without sacrificing flavor with this Crispy Pork recipe, specifically designed for air fryer enthusiasts. A perfect blend of crunch and tenderness awaits in every bite, offering a protein-rich meal that's both satisfying and guilt-free.

Servings: 4

Prepping Time: 15 minutes

Cook Time: 20 minutes

Difficulty: Easy

Ingredients:

- 1 lb pork loin, sliced into thin strips
- 2 tbsp olive oil
- 1 tsp salt
- 1 tsp black pepper
- 1 tsp garlic powder
- 1 tsp smoked paprika

Step-by-Step Preparation:

1. Preheat your air fryer to 400°F.
2. Toss the pork strips with olive oil, salt, pepper, garlic powder, and smoked paprika until evenly coated.
3. Arrange the pork strips in a single layer in the air fryer basket. Work in batches if necessary to avoid overcrowding.
4. Cook for 10 minutes. Flip the strips and cook for another 10 minutes or until crispy and cooked.
5. Let the pork rest for a few minutes before serving.

Nutritional Facts: (Per serving)

- Calories: 290
- Protein: 25g
- Fat: 20g
- Carbohydrates: 0g
- Sodium: 600mg

Elevate your dining experience with this Crispy Pork recipe, a testament to how air fryers can transform simple ingredients into a delectable feast. Whether you're seeking a protein-packed meal or a quick and easy dinner solution, this dish proves that healthy eating can also be delicious and convenient.

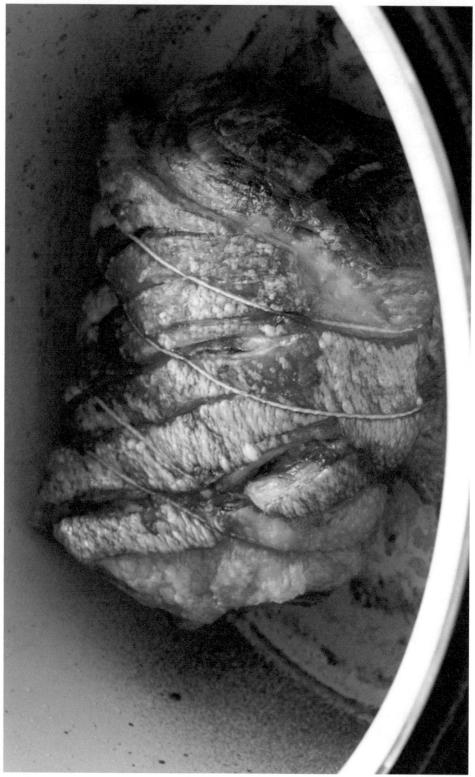

Recipe 12: Pork Shoulder Joint of Meat

Embrace simplicity with this Pork Shoulder recipe, tailor-made for your air fryer. Marrying convenience with traditional flavors, this dish brings forward the essence of homely comfort food, enriched with high protein for those mindful of their nutritional intake. Let's turn a classic favorite into your next culinary adventure, where every bite speaks volumes of tenderness and taste.

Servings: 6

Prepping Time: 10 minutes

Cook Time: 60 minutes

Difficulty: Medium

Ingredients:

- ✓ 3 lbs pork shoulder joint
- ✓ 1 tbsp olive oil
- ✓ 2 tsp salt
- ✓ 1 tsp ground black pepper
- ✓ 1 tsp garlic powder
- ✓ 1 tsp onion powder
- ✓ 1 tsp dried thyme

Step-by-Step Preparation:

1. Preheat your air fryer to 360°F (182°C).

2. Rub the pork shoulder evenly with olive oil. Mix salt, pepper, garlic powder, onion powder, and thyme in a bowl, then coat the pork shoulder with this seasoning mix.

3. Place the seasoned pork shoulder in the air fryer basket. Cook for 30 minutes.

4. After 30 minutes, flip the pork shoulder and cook for 30 minutes, or until the meat reaches an internal temperature of 145°F (63°C).

5. Remove the pork shoulder from the air fryer and let it rest for 10 minutes before slicing.

Nutritional Facts: (Per serving)

- ❖ Calories: 330
- ❖ Protein: 47g
- ❖ Fat: 14g
- ❖ Carbohydrates: 1g
- ❖ Sodium: 830mg

Concluding on a note of satisfaction, this Pork Shoulder recipe reaffirms the joy of cooking with an air fryer. It's a celebration of how technology meets tradition to serve up a dish that's high in protein, rich in flavor, and perfect for any occasion. Let this recipe be a testament to the endless possibilities that await in your kitchen, where every meal is an opportunity to explore, enjoy, and eat well.

Recipe 13: Marinated Pork Belly Slide Meat

Unlock the secret to succulent Marinated Pork Belly, a recipe that promises to delight your palate while fitting perfectly into your high-protein lifestyle. Using an air fryer, this dish achieves an exquisite balance of crispy and tender textures, making every meal an unforgettable experience. Get ready to elevate your culinary skills with a recipe that's as nutritious as delicious.

Servings: 4

Prepping Time: 4 hours 15 minutes (including marination time)

Cook Time: 25 minutes

Difficulty: Medium

Ingredients:

- 1 lb pork belly, sliced
- 1/4 cup soy sauce
- 2 tbsp honey
- 1 tbsp rice vinegar
- 1 tsp garlic, minced
- 1 tsp ginger, minced
- 1/2 tsp ground black pepper
- 1 tsp sesame oil

Step-by-Step Preparation:

1. Combine soy sauce, honey, rice vinegar, minced garlic, ginger, black pepper, and sesame oil in a bowl to create the marinade.

2. Place pork belly slices in the marinade, ensuring each piece is well coated. Cover and refrigerate for at least 4 hours.

3. Preheat your air fryer to 400°F (200°C).

4. Remove the pork belly from the marinade and place it in the air fryer basket in a single layer. Cook for 25 minutes, turning halfway through, until crispy and golden.

5. Allow to cool slightly before serving.

Nutritional Facts: (Per serving)

- Calories: 520
- Protein: 14g
- Fat: 50g
- Carbohydrates: 8g
- Sodium: 800mg

With this Marinated Pork Belly recipe, you'll discover the joy of cooking with an air fryer, transforming simple ingredients into a high-protein feast. Perfect for any day of the week, this dish is a testament to marination's power and air frying's magic. Enjoy the perfect blend of flavors and textures, making every meal a moment to savor.

Recipe 14: Juicy Beef Pepper Steak

Step into the world of gourmet cooking made simple with this Juicy Beef Pepper Steak recipe. Harnessing the power of your air fryer, we're bringing steakhouse quality into your kitchen, complete with a zesty red sharp sauce. This dish not only packs a protein punch but also turns an ordinary meal into an extraordinary dining experience with minimal effort. Get ready to impress with this foolproof method for consistently achieving the perfect medium-rare steak.

Servings: 2

Prepping Time: 20 minutes

Cook Time: 12 minutes

Difficulty: Easy

Ingredients:

- ✓ 2 beef steaks (about 1 inch thick)
- ✓ 1 tbsp olive oil
- ✓ 1 tsp freshly ground black pepper
- ✓ 1 tsp sea salt
- ✓ 1/2 cup red wine
- ✓ 2 tbsp soy sauce
- ✓ 1 tbsp balsamic vinegar
- ✓ 2 cloves garlic, minced
- ✓ 1 tsp honey
- ✓ 1/4 tsp red pepper flakes

Step-by-Step Preparation:

1. Preheat your air fryer to 400°F (200°C).
2. Rub each steak with olive oil and season generously with salt and pepper.
3. Place steaks in the air fryer and cook for 6 minutes. Flip, then cook for an additional 6 minutes for medium-rare. Adjust time for your preferred doneness.
4. While steaks cook, combine red wine, soy sauce, balsamic vinegar, garlic, honey, and red pepper flakes in a small saucepan. Simmer over medium heat until reduced by half, creating a sharp, flavorful sauce.
5. After cooking, rest the steaks for 5 minutes, then serve them with the red sharp sauce drizzled over the top.

Nutritional Facts: (Per serving)

- ❖ Calories: 450
- ❖ Protein: 46g
- ❖ Fat: 28g
- ❖ Carbohydrates: 6g
- ❖ Sodium: 1200mg

Conclude your day on a high note with this Juicy Beef Pepper Steak, a testament to how air fryer cooking can elevate the simplest ingredients into a nourishing and indulgently satisfying meal. This dish caters to your protein needs and indulges your taste buds with its rich, bold flavors. Perfect for a special occasion or a luxurious weeknight dinner, it promises a culinary journey that's as delightful as healthy.

Recipe 15: Meatballs Into an Air Fryer

Whip up a batch of these succulent meatballs using your air fryer for a meal that's not just high in protein but also incredibly flavorful and satisfying. This recipe adds a twist to the classic dish, offering a healthier option without compromising taste. Whether you're looking to impress at a dinner party or want a nutritious meal, these air fryer meatballs will become your go-to recipe.

Servings: 4

Prepping Time: 15 minutes

Cook Time: 15 minutes

Difficulty: Easy

Ingredients:

- ✓ 1 lb ground beef (85% lean)
- ✓ 1/4 cup breadcrumbs
- ✓ 1 large egg
- ✓ 2 cloves garlic, minced
- ✓ 1/4 cup grated Parmesan cheese
- ✓ 1 tsp salt
- ✓ 1/2 tsp ground black pepper
- ✓ 1 tsp Italian seasoning
- ✓ 1 tbsp olive oil

Step-by-Step Preparation:

1. Mix the ground beef, breadcrumbs, egg, garlic, Parmesan cheese, salt, pepper, and Italian seasoning in a large bowl until well combined.
2. Form the mixture into meatballs about 1 inch in diameter.
3. Brush each meatball lightly with olive oil to enhance browning.
4. Preheat the air fryer to 400°F. Place the meatballs in the air fryer basket, ensuring they are not touching.
5. Cook for 15 minutes, turning halfway through, until meatballs are browned and cooked through.
6. Serve hot with your favorite sauce or as part of your main dish.

Nutritional Facts: (Per serving)

- ❖ Calories: 310
- ❖ Protein: 23g
- ❖ Fat: 20g
- ❖ Carbohydrates: 6g
- ❖ Sodium: 720mg

Wrap up your day with these delicious air fryer meatballs, a dish that proves eating well doesn't mean sacrificing flavor. Perfect for any occasion, from casual weeknights to special gatherings, these meatballs are sure to delight. Enjoy the ease and health benefits of air frying, and let these meatballs become a staple in your culinary repertoire.

Recipe 16: Fatty Bacon Strips in Air Fryer

Indulge in the ultimate comfort food with these Fatty Bacon Strips, cooked to perfection in your air fryer. This recipe delivers all the satisfying crunch and flavor you crave, with a protein boost to kickstart your day or complement your favorite dishes. Say goodbye to splattering oil and hello to a cleaner, healthier way to enjoy bacon at its best.

Servings: 4

Prepping Time: 5 minutes

Cook Time: 10 minutes

Difficulty: Easy

Ingredients:

- ✓ 8 thick-cut bacon strips

Step-by-Step Preparation:

1. Preheat your air fryer to 360°F (182°C).

2. Arrange the bacon strips in a single layer in the air fryer basket. If your basket is small, you may need to cook in batches to avoid overcrowding.

3. Cook for 10 minutes or until the bacon reaches your desired level of crispiness. Halfway through cooking, flip the bacon strips to ensure even cooking.

4. Once cooked, transfer the bacon strips to a paper towel-lined plate to absorb any excess fat.

Nutritional Facts: (Per serving)

- ❖ Calories: 250
- ❖ Protein: 18g
- ❖ Fat: 20g
- ❖ Carbohydrates: 0g
- ❖ Sodium: 800mg

Celebrate the simple pleasures with these Fatty Bacon Strips, a delightful twist on a breakfast classic made more accessible and healthier with your air fryer. Whether assembling an epic brunch or adding a crispy topping to salads and burgers, this recipe offers the perfect blend of convenience and flavor. Embrace the joy of effortless cooking and elevate your meals with savory goodness.

Recipe 17: Sausages Fried With Spices & Herbs

Savor the rich flavors of Sausages Fried with Spices and Herbs, a recipe that transforms simple sausages into a culinary masterpiece. This dish combines the ease of air frying with a medley of herbs and spices, ensuring each bite is bursting with flavor. Ideal for a protein-packed meal or a hearty snack, these sausages promise to be a hit among all who try them.

Servings: 4

Prepping Time: 10 minutes

Cook Time: 15 minutes

Difficulty: Easy

Ingredients:

- ✓ 8 pork sausages
- ✓ 1 tsp paprika
- ✓ 1/2 tsp garlic powder
- ✓ 1/2 tsp onion powder
- ✓ 1/4 tsp ground black pepper
- ✓ 1/4 tsp dried thyme
- ✓ 1/4 tsp dried oregano
- ✓ 1 tbsp olive oil

Step-by-Step Preparation:

1. Mix paprika, garlic powder, onion powder, black pepper, thyme, and oregano in a small bowl.

2. Lightly brush each sausage with olive oil, then evenly coat with the spice mixture.

3. Preheat the air fryer to 400°F (200°C).

4. Arrange the sausages in the air fryer basket, ensuring they are not touching for even cooking.

5. Cook for 15 minutes, turning halfway through, until the sausages are browned and cooked through.

Nutritional Facts: (Per serving)

- ❖ Calories: 320
- ❖ Protein: 19g
- ❖ Fat: 26g
- ❖ Carbohydrates: 2g
- ❖ Sodium: 780mg

End your day on a high note with these flavorful Sausages Fried with Spices and Herbs, a testament to the versatility and convenience of air frying. Whether you're looking for an effortless weeknight dinner or a delicious way to increase your protein intake, this dish will satisfy your cravings and spice up your meal routine.

Recipe 18: Grilled Lamb Mutton Meat Chops Steaks

Discover the rich, succulent flavors of Grilled Lamb Mutton Meat Chops, a recipe designed to bring out the best in your air fryer. This high-protein dish marries the robust taste of lamb with a perfect blend of seasonings, delivering a restaurant-quality meal at home. Quickly prepared and packed with flavor, these lamb chops will become a new favorite in your culinary repertoire.

Servings: 4

Prepping Time: 15 minutes

Cook Time: 12 minutes

Difficulty: Medium

Ingredients:

- ✓ 4 lamb mutton chops
- ✓ 2 tbsp olive oil
- ✓ 1 tsp rosemary, chopped
- ✓ 1 tsp thyme, chopped
- ✓ 2 cloves garlic, minced
- ✓ Salt and freshly ground black pepper to taste

Step-by-Step Preparation:

1. Rinse the lamb chops and pat dry with paper towels.
2. Combine olive oil, rosemary, thyme, and garlic in a small bowl. Rub this mixture over lamb chops, then season with salt and pepper.
3. Let the chops marinate for at least 10 minutes at room temperature.
4. Preheat the air fryer to 400°F (200°C).
5. Place the lamb chops in the air fryer basket, ensuring they are not overlapping.
6. Cook for 6 minutes, flip the chops, and cook for 6 minutes for medium-rare, or adjust the cooking time to your preference.
7. Let the chops rest for a few minutes before serving.

Nutritional Facts: (Per serving)

- ❖ Calories: 410
- ❖ Protein: 24g
- ❖ Fat: 35g
- ❖ Carbohydrates: 0g
- ❖ Sodium: 75mg

Cap off your day with these Grilled Lamb Mutton Meat Chops, a testament to the simplicity and elegance of cooking with an air fryer. Ideal for a special dinner or a nutritious weeknight meal, these chops offer a gourmet experience that's effortlessly achieved. Dive into the depths of flavor and enjoy a high-protein feast that's as satisfying as it is healthy.

Recipe 19: Roast Leg of Lamb With Potatoes and Rosemary

Experience the joy of bringing a classic feast to your table with this Roast Leg of Lamb with Potatoes and Rosemary recipe. Utilizing the air fryer, this dish simplifies gourmet cooking, blending the rich flavors of lamb with the rustic taste of rosemary potatoes. Perfect for a family dinner or a special occasion, it's a high-protein meal that doesn't compromise flavor or nutrition.

Servings: 6

Prepping Time: 20 minutes

Cook Time: 60 minutes

Difficulty: Medium

Ingredients:

- ✓ 1 leg of lamb (about 4-5 lbs)
- ✓ 4 tbsp olive oil
- ✓ 4 cloves garlic, minced
- ✓ 2 tbsp fresh rosemary, chopped
- ✓ Salt and pepper to taste
- ✓ 1.5 lbs small potatoes, halved
- ✓ 1 tsp dried thyme

Step-by-Step Preparation:

1. Rub the leg of lamb with 2 tbsp of olive oil, garlic, 1 tbsp of rosemary, salt, and pepper. Let it marinate for at least 15 minutes.
2. Preheat the air fryer to 360°F (182°C).
3. Place the lamb in the air fryer basket and cook for 50 minutes or until it reaches your desired level of doneness.
4. Toss the potatoes with olive oil, rosemary, thyme, salt, and pepper.
5. After the lamb has cooked for 30 minutes, add the potatoes to the air fryer and continue cooking for the remaining 20 minutes, or until the potatoes are tender and the lamb is cooked.
6. Let the lamb rest for 10 minutes before slicing. Serve with the roasted rosemary potatoes on the side.

Nutritional Facts: (Per serving)

- ❖ Calories: 560
- ❖ Protein: 48g
- ❖ Fat: 32g
- ❖ Carbohydrates: 22g
- ❖ Sodium: 120mg

Wrap up your culinary adventure with this Roast Leg of Lamb with Potatoes and Rosemary, showcasing how the air fryer can elevate traditional recipes into something truly spectacular. This dish celebrates flavors and textures, proving that healthy, high-protein meals can be profoundly satisfying and delicious. Enjoy the best of both worlds with this easy-to-follow recipe that's sure to impress.

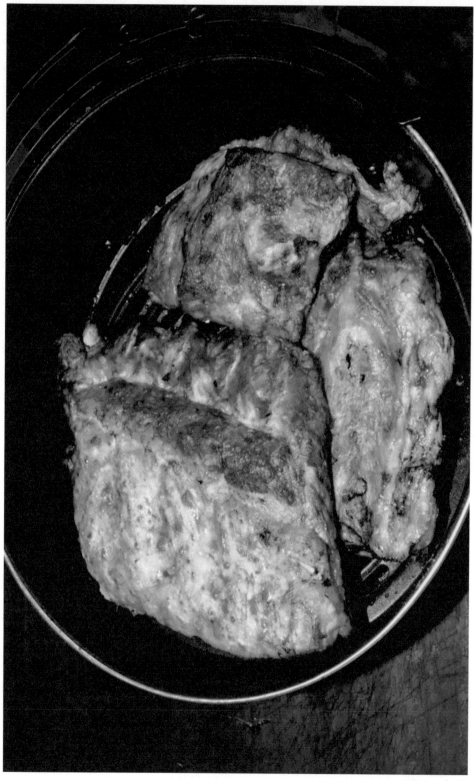

Recipe 20: Cooked Spare Ribs in Air Fryer With Meat Side Up

Indulge in the mouthwatering delight of Cooked Spare Ribs, prepared in your air fryer with the meat side up to ensure a juicy, flavorful experience. This high-protein recipe brings a new convenience to cooking ribs, combining the classic taste you love with a quicker, healthier method. Perfect for meat lovers looking to enjoy a tender, fall-off-the-bone feast without the fuss.

Servings: 4

Prepping Time: 10 minutes

Cook Time: 40 minutes

Difficulty: Easy

Ingredients:

- ✓ 2 lbs pork spare ribs
- ✓ 2 tbsp barbecue sauce
- ✓ 1 tbsp brown sugar
- ✓ 1 tsp paprika
- ✓ 1 tsp garlic powder
- ✓ 1 tsp onion powder
- ✓ 1/2 tsp ground black pepper
- ✓ 1/2 tsp salt

Step-by-Step Preparation:

1. Mix barbecue sauce, brown sugar, paprika, garlic powder, onion powder, black pepper, and salt in a small bowl.

2. Rub this mixture all over the spare ribs, ensuring they are well coated.

3. Preheat the air fryer to 380°F (193°C).

4. Place the ribs in the air fryer basket, meat side up, and cook for 40 minutes. Halfway through, brush the ribs with additional barbecue sauce for extra flavor.

5. Once cooked, let the ribs rest for a few minutes before serving.

Nutritional Facts: (Per serving)

- ❖ Calories: 580
- ❖ Protein: 35g
- ❖ Fat: 44g
- ❖ Carbohydrates: 12g
- ❖ Sodium: 610mg

Conclude your day with these effortlessly succulent Spare Ribs, a testament to the simplicity and power of air frying. Whether a casual family dinner or a special gathering, this recipe promises flavor, tenderness, and satisfaction. Enjoy the perfect ribs every time, with minimal preparation and maximum enjoyment.

Chapter 03: Seafood Strength

← —————————————————————————— →

Recipe 21: Crispy Fish With Herbs & Spices

Dive into the flavors of the sea with our Crispy Baked Fish seasoned with exotic herbs and spices for an irresistible meal. This high-protein recipe is perfect for health-conscious seafood lovers, utilizing the air fryer for that ideal crispiness.

Servings: 4

Cook Time: 20 minutes

Prepping Time: 15 minutes

Difficulty: Easy

Ingredients:

- ✓ 4 fillets of your choice of fish
- ✓ 2 tablespoons olive oil
- ✓ 1 teaspoon paprika
- ✓ 1 teaspoon garlic powder
- ✓ 1/2 teaspoon dried oregano
- ✓ 1/2 teaspoon dried thyme
- ✓ Salt and pepper to taste
- ✓ Lemon wedges for serving

Step-by-Step Preparation:

1. Preheat the air fryer to 400°F (200°C).
2. Rinse the fish fillets and pat dry with paper towels.
3. Mix olive oil, paprika, garlic powder, oregano, thyme, salt, and pepper in a small bowl.
4. Brush the spice mixture over both sides of the fish fillets.
5. Place the fillets in the air fryer basket, ensuring they don't overlap.
6. Cook for 10 minutes, flip, and continue cooking for another 10 minutes or until crispy and cooked.
7. Serve hot with lemon wedges on the side.

Nutritional Facts: (Per serving)

- ❖ Calories: 200
- ❖ Protein: 22g
- ❖ Fat: 10g
- ❖ Carbohydrates: 0g
- ❖ Sodium: 120mg

Wrap up your culinary adventure with this Crispy Baked Fish that brings flavor and nutrition to your table. Whether you're a seafood lover or trying to incorporate more protein into your diet, this air fryer recipe offers a delicious and healthy twist to your regular fish dish.

Recipe 22: Grilled Salmon and Vegetables

Savor the simplicity and richness of Grilled Salmon and Vegetables, a high-protein dish that combines the health benefits of seafood with the freshness of garden picks. This air fryer recipe ensures a delightful crunch and flavor, making it a perfect meal for any day of the week.

Servings: 4

Cook Time: 15 minutes

Prepping Time: 20 minutes

Difficulty: Medium

Ingredients:

- ✓ 4 salmon fillets (about 6 ounces each)
- ✓ 2 tablespoons olive oil
- ✓ 1 teaspoon salt
- ✓ 1/2 teaspoon black pepper
- ✓ 1 zucchini, sliced
- ✓ 1 bell pepper, cut into pieces
- ✓ 1 red onion, cut into wedges
- ✓ 2 tablespoons lemon juice
- ✓ 1 teaspoon dried dill

Step-by-Step Preparation:

1. Preheat your air fryer to 400°F (200°C).
2. Brush both the salmon and vegetables with olive oil. Season with salt and pepper.
3. Arrange the salmon and vegetables in the air fryer basket in a single layer. You may need to cook in batches to avoid overcrowding.
4. Cook for 12-15 minutes until the salmon is cooked and the vegetables are tender and slightly charred.
5. Drizzle lemon juice over the cooked salmon and vegetables and sprinkle with dried dill before serving.

Nutritional Facts: (Per serving)

- ❖ Calories: 310
- ❖ Protein: 34g
- ❖ Fat: 17g
- ❖ Carbohydrates: 8g
- ❖ Fiber: 2g
- ❖ Sodium: 650mg

End your day on a high note with this Grilled Salmon and Vegetables recipe. It's a heart-healthy, protein-packed meal that brings the best out of simple ingredients with minimal prep and cooking time. Perfect for a nutritious weeknight dinner or a casual weekend gathering, this dish is sure to impress.

Recipe 23: Roasted Dorado or Sea Bream Fish

Indulge in the delicate flavors of the sea with our Roasted Dorado or Sea Bream, adorned with citrus slices, aromatic spices, fresh rosemary, and spinach. This air fryer recipe elevates the humble fish into a gourmet delight, offering a protein-rich meal that's as nutritious as it is flavorful.

Servings: 4

Prepping Time: 10 minutes

Cook Time: 18 minutes

Difficulty: Easy

Ingredients:

- ✓ 4 dorado or sea bream fillets
- ✓ 1 lemon, sliced
- ✓ 1 orange, sliced
- ✓ 1 teaspoon salt
- ✓ 1/2 teaspoon black pepper
- ✓ 2 tablespoons olive oil
- ✓ 1 tablespoon fresh rosemary leaves
- ✓ 2 cups fresh spinach
- ✓ 1 teaspoon paprika

Step-by-Step Preparation:

1. Preheat the air fryer to 390°F (200°C).
2. Season the fish fillets with salt, pepper, and paprika. Drizzle with olive oil.
3. Place a layer of lemon and orange slices in the air fryer basket. Top with the fish fillets.
4. Sprinkle fresh rosemary over the fillets.
5. Arrange the spinach around the fish.
6. Cook for 18 minutes or until the fish flakes easily with a fork.
7. Serve immediately, garnished with additional citrus slices if desired.

Nutritional Facts: **(Per serving)**

- ❖ Calories: 240
- ❖ Protein: 35g
- ❖ Fat: 10g
- ❖ Carbohydrates: 5g
- ❖ Fiber: 2g
- ❖ Sodium: 630mg

Conclude your meal with a sense of accomplishment after crafting this Roasted Dorado or Sea Bream. This dish satisfies your seafood cravings and packs a punch of protein and vital nutrients. Perfect for a special occasion or a wholesome family dinner, it's sure to bring a splash of culinary excitement to your table.

Recipe 24: Air Fryer Snakeskin Gourami Fish

Experience the exotic flavors of Southeast Asia with our Air Fryer Snakeskin Gourami, a delicacy known for its tender texture and unique taste. This high-protein recipe offers a healthier twist on the traditional fried fish, promising a delicious meal that's both nutritious and satisfying.

Servings: 4

Prepping Time: 10 minutes

Cook Time: 20 minutes

Difficulty: Medium

Ingredients:

- ✓ 4 Snakeskin gourami fish, cleaned and scored
- ✓ 1 tablespoon turmeric powder
- ✓ 2 teaspoons salt
- ✓ 1 teaspoon pepper
- ✓ 2 tablespoons coconut oil
- ✓ 1 lime, for serving
- ✓ Fresh cilantro for garnish

Step-by-Step Preparation:

1. Preheat the air fryer to 400°F (200°C).
2. Rub the fish with turmeric, salt, and pepper evenly on both sides and inside the scores.
3. Brush the air fryer basket with coconut oil and place the fish in the basket.
4. Cook for 20 minutes or until the fish is golden and crispy. Flip halfway through the cooking time.
5. Serve hot, garnished with lime wedges and fresh cilantro.

Nutritional Facts: **(Per serving)**

- ❖ Calories: 220
- ❖ Protein: 23g
- ❖ Fat: 13g
- ❖ Carbohydrates: 1g
- ❖ Sodium: 590mg

Concluding with a crisp and flavorful note, this Air Fryer Snakeskin Gourami brings a touch of the exotic to your dining table. It's a simple yet elegant dish that showcases the versatility of air frying, turning an ordinary meal into a gourmet experience. Perfect for those looking to enjoy traditional flavors with a modern, healthy twist.

Recipe 25: Grilled Spicy Salmon Pieces

Embark on a fiery culinary journey with our Grilled Spicy Salmon, a dish that promises to awaken your taste buds. Prepared in an air fryer, this high-protein seafood recipe combines the rich flavors of salmon with a blend of spices, offering a healthy yet indulgent meal option that's quick and easy to make.

Servings: 4

Prepping Time: 15 minutes

Cook Time: 12 minutes

Difficulty: Easy

Ingredients:

- ✓ 4 salmon fillets (about 6 oz each)
- ✓ 2 tablespoons olive oil
- ✓ 1 teaspoon paprika
- ✓ 1 teaspoon garlic powder
- ✓ 1/2 teaspoon cayenne pepper
- ✓ 1/2 teaspoon dried thyme
- ✓ Salt and black pepper to taste
- ✓ Lemon wedges for serving

Step-by-Step Preparation:

1. Preheat the air fryer to 400°F (200°C).
2. Mix olive oil, paprika, garlic powder, cayenne pepper, thyme, salt, and black pepper in a small bowl.
3. Brush the spice mixture generously on both sides of the salmon fillets.
4. Place the salmon in the air fryer basket, skin-side down.
5. Cook for 12 minutes or until the salmon is cooked and the edges are slightly crispy.
6. Serve immediately with lemon wedges on the side.

Nutritional Facts: (Per serving)

- ❖ Calories: 280
- ❖ Protein: 23g
- ❖ Fat: 20g
- ❖ Carbohydrates: 1g
- ❖ Sodium: 75mg

Wrap up your day with this grilled spicy salmon, the perfect blend of flavor and nutrition. Ideal for those seeking a quick, delicious, and protein-rich meal, this air fryer recipe proves that healthy eating doesn't have to be bland or time-consuming. Enjoy the simplicity of perfectly cooked salmon with a spicy twist.

Recipe 26: Golden Air Fried Shrimp With Cocktail Sacue

Delight in the crispy, golden goodness of Air Fried Shrimp, served with a tangy cocktail sauce. This recipe brings the classic fried shrimp experience to your kitchen without the extra oil, using an air fryer to achieve that perfect crunch. It's a high-protein, low-fat seafood option that's as enjoyable to make as it is to eat.

Servings: 4

Prepping Time: 10 minutes

Cook Time: 8 minutes

Difficulty: Easy

Ingredients:

- ✓ 1 pound large shrimp, peeled and deveined
- ✓ 1 teaspoon garlic powder
- ✓ 1/2 teaspoon paprika
- ✓ Salt and pepper to taste
- ✓ 1 tablespoon olive oil
- ✓ For the cocktail sauce:
    - ○ 1/2 cup ketchup
    - ○ 2 tablespoons horseradish
    - ○ 1 tablespoon lemon juice
    - ○ 1 teaspoon Worcestershire sauce
    - ○ A dash of hot sauce (optional)

Step-by-Step Preparation:

1. Preheat the air fryer to 400°F (200°C).
2. Toss the shrimp with garlic powder, paprika, salt, pepper, and olive oil until evenly coated.
3. Arrange the shrimp in a single layer in the air fryer basket. You may need to cook in batches to avoid overcrowding.
4. Cook for 8 minutes, flipping halfway through, or until golden shrimp are cooked.
5. While the shrimp is cooked, mix ketchup, horseradish, lemon juice, Worcestershire sauce, and hot sauce (if using) in a small bowl to make the cocktail sauce.
6. Serve the shrimp hot with the cocktail sauce on the side.

Nutritional Facts: **(Per serving)**

- ❖ Calories: 180
- ❖ Protein: 24g
- ❖ Fat: 4g
- ❖ Carbohydrates: 12g
- ❖ Sodium: 870mg

End your search for the perfect appetizer or main dish with this Golden Air Fried Shrimp. It's a testament to how simple ingredients can create a feast for the senses when combined with the magic of air frying. This dish satisfies your seafood cravings and adds a healthy twist to a beloved classic.

Recipe 27: Grill Sea Bass

Savor the light, nutritious flavors of Grilled Sea Bass with Vegetable Salads, a dish that marries the tenderness of fish with the crisp freshness of seasonal vegetables. Cooked in an air fryer to perfection, this high-protein recipe is a testament to healthy eating without compromising taste or texture. A perfect choice for those looking for a wholesome, satisfying meal.

Servings: 4

Prepping Time: 15 minutes

Cook Time: 12 minutes

Difficulty: Medium

Ingredients:

- ✓ 4 sea bass fillets (about 6 oz each)
- ✓ 2 tablespoons olive oil
- ✓ Salt and pepper to taste
- ✓ 1 lemon, sliced
- ✓ 1 zucchini, sliced into rounds
- ✓ 1 yellow bell pepper, sliced
- ✓ 1 red onion, sliced
- ✓ 2 cups mixed greens
- ✓ 1 tablespoon balsamic vinegar

Step-by-Step Preparation:

1. Preheat the air fryer to 390°F (200°C).
2. Season the sea bass fillets with salt, pepper, and olive oil. Place a few lemon slices on each fillet.
3. Toss the zucchini, bell pepper, and red onion with the remaining olive oil, salt, and pepper in a bowl.
4. Place the fillets and vegetable slices in the air fryer basket, ensuring they are not overcrowded.
5. Cook for 12 minutes or until the fish is opaque and vegetables are tender.
6. Toss the cooked vegetables with mixed greens and balsamic vinegar to create a salad.
7. Serve the grilled sea bass on a bed of vegetable salad.

Nutritional Facts: (Per serving)

- ❖ Calories: 280
- ❖ Protein: 25g
- ❖ Fat: 16g
- ❖ Carbohydrates: 8g
- ❖ Fiber: 2g
- ❖ Sodium: 120mg

Finish your meal on a high note with this Grilled Sea Bass with Vegetable Salads. It celebrates simple ingredients, each contributing unique flavors and textures to create a balanced, nutritious dish. Perfect for any day of the week, this recipe is a delightful way to enjoy the benefits of a high-protein, vegetable-rich diet.

Recipe 28: Lobster, Shrimp and Fish

Dive into a seafood extravaganza with our Lobster, Shrimp, and Fish trio, a luxurious yet simple dish that brings the ocean's bounty straight to your plate. Prepared in the air fryer for a healthier twist, this high-protein feast celebrates the delicate flavors of the sea, promising a dining experience that's both nutritious and indulgent.

Servings: 4

Prepping Time: 20 minutes

Cook Time: 15 minutes

Difficulty: Medium

Ingredients:

- ✓ 2 lobster tails, split
- ✓ 8 large shrimp, peeled and deveined
- ✓ 4 fish fillets (your choice), about 6 oz each
- ✓ 2 tablespoons olive oil
- ✓ 1 teaspoon garlic powder
- ✓ 1 teaspoon paprika
- ✓ Salt and pepper to taste
- ✓ Lemon wedges for serving
- ✓ Fresh parsley, chopped, for garnish

Step-by-Step Preparation:

1. Preheat the air fryer to 400°F (200°C).

2. Brush the lobster tails, shrimp, and fish fillets with olive oil. Season with garlic powder, paprika, salt, and pepper.

3. Arrange the seafood in the air fryer basket in a single layer. You may need to cook in batches.

4. Cook for 15 minutes until the seafood is cooked and slightly golden.

5. Serve immediately, garnished with lemon wedges and fresh parsley.

Nutritional Facts: (Per serving)

- ❖ Calories: 320
- ❖ Protein: 46g
- ❖ Fat: 12g
- ❖ Carbohydrates: 2g
- ❖ Sodium: 320mg

Conclude your meal on a luxurious note with this Lobster, Shrimp, and Fish dish. This recipe combines the best of the sea in one plate, perfect for a special occasion or when you're in the mood to treat yourself. Enjoy the ease of cooking and the symphony of flavors that air frying brings to seafood, making every bite a celebration.

Recipe 29: River Shrimp Cooked in Air Fryer

Embark on a culinary journey with our River Shrimp Cooked in Air Fryer, a simple yet sophisticated recipe that brings the fresh flavors of the river to your kitchen. This high-protein seafood delight leverages the convenience and health benefits of air frying, offering a crispy, flavorful dish that will impress seafood lovers and home chefs alike.

Servings: 4

Prepping Time: 10 minutes

Cook Time: 10 minutes

Difficulty: Easy

Ingredients:

- ✓ 1 pound river shrimp, cleaned and deveined
- ✓ 1 tablespoon olive oil
- ✓ 1 teaspoon smoked paprika
- ✓ 1/2 teaspoon garlic powder
- ✓ Salt and pepper to taste
- ✓ Lemon wedges for serving
- ✓ Fresh parsley, finely chopped, for garnish

Step-by-Step Preparation:

1. Preheat the air fryer to 400°F (200°C).
2. Toss the shrimp with olive oil, smoked paprika, garlic powder, salt, and pepper until evenly coated.
3. Arrange the shrimp in a single layer in the air fryer basket. You may need to work in batches to avoid overcrowding.
4. Cook for 10 minutes or until the shrimp are golden and crisp.
5. Serve hot, garnished with lemon wedges and a sprinkle of fresh parsley.

Nutritional Facts: (Per serving)

- ❖ Calories: 120
- ❖ Protein: 23g
- ❖ Fat: 3g
- ❖ Carbohydrates: 1g
- ❖ Sodium: 200mg

Conclude your dining experience on a high note with this River Shrimp recipe. It's a testament to how easy and quick it is to enjoy a gourmet seafood meal at home. Perfect for a nutritious weeknight dinner or a special occasion, this dish is a delicious way to enjoy the benefits of air frying, leaving you satisfied yet craving more.

Recipe 30: Crispy and Spicy Anchovy Fry

Indulge in the flavors of the ocean with our Crispy and Spicy Anchovy Fry, a delightful recipe that transforms tiny anchovies into a crispy, spicy sensation. Marinated with an array of spices and cooked to perfection in an air fryer, this high-protein dish is a testament to the magic of simple ingredients coming together to create something extraordinary.

Servings: 4

Cook Time: 8 minutes

Prepping Time: 30 minutes (including marination)

Difficulty: Easy

Ingredients:

- ✓ 1 pound fresh anchovies, cleaned
- ✓ 2 tablespoons olive oil
- ✓ 1 teaspoon turmeric powder
- ✓ 1 teaspoon chili powder
- ✓ 1/2 teaspoon ground coriander
- ✓ 1/2 teaspoon garlic powder
- ✓ Salt to taste
- ✓ Lemon wedges for serving

Step-by-Step Preparation:

1. Mix olive oil, turmeric, chili powder, ground coriander, garlic powder, and salt in a bowl.

2. Add the anchovies to the marinade and toss well to coat evenly. Let it marinate for 20 minutes.

3. Preheat the air fryer to 400°F (200°C).

4. Arrange the marinated anchovies in a single layer in the air fryer basket. Avoid overcrowding for even cooking.

5. Cook for 8 minutes or until the anchovies are crispy and golden.

6. Serve immediately, accompanied by lemon wedges, for a tangy kick.

Nutritional Facts: **(Per serving)**

- ❖ Calories: 198
- ❖ Protein: 25g
- ❖ Fat: 10g
- ❖ Carbohydrates: 1g
- ❖ Sodium: 75mg

Conclude your meal with this Crispy and Spicy Anchovy Fry, a dish sure to spark conversation and delight your taste buds. It's a celebration of bold flavors and the nutritional bounty of the sea, offering a perfect blend of health and taste. Whether as an appetizer or a main dish, these anchovies are bound to be a memorable part of your culinary repertoire.

Chapter 04: Veggie Power

Recipe 31: Cauliflower Grilled With Air Fryer

Discover the delicious simplicity of cauliflower grilled to perfection with your air fryer. This high-protein vegetable recipe brings out the best in cauliflower, making it a crunchy, golden delight.

Servings: 4

Cook Time: 15 minutes

Prepping Time: 10 minutes

Difficulty: Easy

Ingredients:

- ✓ 1 large head cauliflower, cut into florets
- ✓ 2 tablespoons olive oil
- ✓ 1 teaspoon garlic powder
- ✓ 1 teaspoon smoked paprika
- ✓ Salt and pepper, to taste
- ✓ 2 tablespoons grated Parmesan (optional)
- ✓ Fresh parsley for garnish

Step-by-Step Preparation:

1. Preheat your air fryer to 380°F (190°C).

2. In a large bowl, toss the cauliflower florets with olive oil, garlic powder, smoked paprika, salt, and pepper until evenly coated.

3. Arrange the cauliflower in the air fryer basket in a single layer; cook for 15 minutes, shaking halfway through.

4. Once golden and tender, sprinkle with grated Parmesan and garnish with fresh parsley before serving.

Nutritional Facts: (Per serving)

- ❖ Calories: 110
- ❖ Protein: 4g
- ❖ Carbohydrates: 10g
- ❖ Fat: 7g
- ❖ Fiber: 4g
- ❖ Sodium: 210mg

Savor the healthful charm of air-fried cauliflower, a high-protein feast that's as nutritious as delicious. Perfect for a quick side dish or a guilt-free snack, it's a testament to the versatility of vegetables when cooked right.

Recipe 32: Air Fried Tandoori Cauliflower

Embrace the vibrant flavors of India with Air Fried Tandoori Cauliflower. This high-protein, air-fryer vegetable recipe transforms cauliflower into a smoky, spicy delicacy, marinated in yogurt and a blend of tandoori spices, then air-fried to perfection for a healthy, flavor-packed treat.

Servings: 4

Prepping Time: 15 minutes (plus marinating time)

Cook Time: 20 minutes

Difficulty: Intermediate

Ingredients:

- 1 large head of cauliflower, cut into florets
- 1 cup plain Greek yogurt
- 2 tablespoons tandoori masala
- 1 teaspoon turmeric
- 1 teaspoon ground cumin
- 1 teaspoon garlic paste
- 1 teaspoon ginger paste
- Salt to taste
- Fresh cilantro for garnish
- Lemon wedges for serving

Step-by-Step Preparation:

1. Mix the yogurt, tandoori masala, turmeric, cumin, garlic paste, ginger paste, and salt in a large bowl.

2. Add the cauliflower florets to the marinade, ensuring each piece is well coated. Let it marinate for at least 30 minutes or overnight for deeper flavor.

3. Preheat your air fryer to 400°F (200°C).

4. Arrange the marinated cauliflower in the air fryer basket in a single layer; air fry for 20 minutes, turning halfway through until the edges are crispy and browned.

5. Garnish with fresh cilantro and serve with lemon wedges on the side.

Nutritional Facts: (Per serving)

- Calories: 123
- Protein: 9g
- Carbohydrates: 15g
- Fat: 3g
- Fiber: 5g
- Sodium: 87mg

Delight in the tangy, spicy flavors of Air Fried Tandoori Cauliflower, a dish that brings the essence of Indian cuisine to your kitchen. This high-protein, vegetarian delight satisfies your taste buds and adds a nutritious punch to your mealtime, proving healthy eating can be irresistibly delicious.

Recipe 33: Fried Tofu

Dive into a world of flavor with Fried Tofu with Sesame and Greens, a dish that perfectly combines the crispiness of air-fried tofu with the earthiness of greens; all brought together with a hint of sesame. This high-protein, air fryer vegetable recipe is not only delicious but also a nutritional powerhouse, ready to impress with its simplicity and depth of flavor.

Servings: 4

Prepping Time: 15 minutes

Cook Time: 20 minutes

Difficulty: Easy

Ingredients:

- ✓ 14 oz (400g) firm tofu, pressed and cubed
- ✓ 2 tablespoons soy sauce
- ✓ 1 tablespoon sesame oil
- ✓ 2 teaspoons cornstarch
- ✓ 1 teaspoon garlic powder

- ✓ 1/4 cup sesame seeds
- ✓ 4 cups mixed greens (spinach, kale, and arugula)
- ✓ Salt and pepper to taste
- ✓ 1 tablespoon olive oil for greens

Step-by-Step Preparation:

1. In a bowl, toss tofu cubes with soy sauce, sesame oil, cornstarch, and garlic powder until evenly coated.

2. Preheat the air fryer to 380°F (190°C). Place the tofu in the basket and air fry for 20 minutes, shaking halfway through, until golden and crispy.

3. In the last 5 minutes of cooking, sprinkle sesame seeds over the tofu to coat evenly and continue air frying.

4. While tofu cooks, heat olive oil in a pan over medium heat. Sauté mixed greens until just wilted, seasoning with salt and pepper.

5. Serve the crispy tofu over the bed of greens, garnished with extra sesame seeds if desired.

Nutritional Facts: (Per serving)

- ❖ Calories: 220
- ❖ Protein: 15g
- ❖ Carbohydrates: 8g

- ❖ Fat: 15g
- ❖ Fiber: 3g
- ❖ Sodium: 320mg

Enjoy the delightful crunch of Fried Tofu with Sesame and Greens, a recipe that's as nourishing as it is flavorful. This easy-to-make, high-protein dish is a testament to the versatility of tofu and the delicious potential of healthy eating, making it a perfect choice for anyone looking to add a touch of excitement to their meals.

Recipe 34: Sweet Potato With Spices and Herbs

Step into a savory world where sweet potato meets a symphony of spices and herbs, all crisped to perfection in your air fryer. This high-protein, air fryer vegetable recipe is a delightful twist on a classic favorite, blending the natural sweetness of sweet potatoes with a bold spice mix for a dish that's as nutritious as it is flavorful.

Servings: 4

Prepping Time: 10 minutes

Cook Time: 25 minutes

Difficulty: Easy

Ingredients:

- ✓ 2 large sweet potatoes, peeled and cubed
- ✓ 1 tablespoon olive oil
- ✓ 1 teaspoon smoked paprika
- ✓ 1/2 teaspoon garlic powder
- ✓ 1/2 teaspoon onion powder
- ✓ 1/4 teaspoon cayenne pepper
- ✓ 1 teaspoon dried thyme
- ✓ Salt and pepper to taste
- ✓ Fresh parsley, chopped for garnish

Step-by-Step Preparation:

1. In a large bowl, toss sweet potato cubes with olive oil, smoked paprika, garlic powder, onion powder, cayenne pepper, dried thyme, salt, and pepper until well coated.

2. Preheat the air fryer to 400°F (200°C).

3. Arrange the sweet potatoes in the air fryer basket in a single layer, ensuring they're not overcrowded for even cooking.

4. Air fry for 25 minutes, shaking the basket halfway through, until the sweet potatoes are golden and crispy.

5. Garnish with fresh parsley before serving.

Nutritional Facts: (Per serving)

- ❖ Calories: 123
- ❖ Protein: 2g
- ❖ Carbohydrates: 26g
- ❖ Fat: 2g
- ❖ Fiber: 4g
- ❖ Sodium: 76mg

Indulge in the comforting warmth of Sweet Potato with Spices and Herbs, a dish that marries the natural sweetness of sweet potatoes with the vibrant flavors of spices and herbs for a truly unforgettable meal. This easy, nutritious recipe is a testament to the versatility and appeal of vegetables when prepared with care and creativity.

Recipe 35: Roasted Parsnips With Honey Mustard Glaze

Explore the unique flavors of Roasted Parsnips with Honey Mustard Glaze, a dish that perfectly balances the earthiness of parsnips with the sweet and tangy flavors of honey and mustard. This high-protein, air fryer vegetable recipe is a delightful side dish that offers a new take on a root vegetable often overshadowed by its carrot cousin, bringing a gourmet twist to your dining table.

Servings: 4

Prepping Time: 15 minutes

Cook Time: 20 minutes

Difficulty: Easy

Ingredients:

- ✓ 4 large parsnips, peeled and sliced into sticks
- ✓ 2 tablespoons olive oil
- ✓ Salt and pepper to taste
- ✓ 2 tablespoons honey
- ✓ 1 tablespoon Dijon mustard
- ✓ 1 teaspoon apple cider vinegar
- ✓ 1/2 teaspoon garlic powder
- ✓ Fresh thyme for garnish

Step-by-Step Preparation:

1. Toss a bowl of parsnip sticks with olive oil, salt, and pepper.
2. Preheat the air fryer to 400°F (200°C).
3. Arrange the parsnips in the air fryer basket in a single layer; air fry for 20 minutes, shaking halfway through, until golden and tender.
4. Meanwhile, whisk together honey, Dijon mustard, apple cider vinegar, and garlic powder in a small bowl.
5. Once parsnips are cooked, toss them in the honey mustard glaze until well coated.
6. Garnish with fresh thyme before serving.

Nutritional Facts: (Per serving)

- ❖ Calories: 190
- ❖ Protein: 2g
- ❖ Carbohydrates: 33g
- ❖ Fat: 7g
- ❖ Fiber: 6g
- ❖ Sodium: 125mg

Delight in the sweet and savory elegance of Roasted Parsnips with Honey Mustard Glaze, a recipe that's as nourishing as it is flavorful. This simple yet sophisticated dish showcases the humble parsnip in a new light, proving that even the most overlooked vegetables can star in a healthy and delicious meal.

Recipe 36: Roasted Champignons With Onions

Savor the simplicity and richness of Roasted Sliced Champignons with Onions, a dish where mushrooms and onions mingle in a dance of flavors, enhanced by roasting in the air fryer. This high-protein, air fryer vegetable recipe highlights the natural umami of mushrooms, paired with the sweetness of onions, making it an irresistible side dish or a healthy snack.

Servings: 4

Prepping Time: 10 minutes

Cook Time: 15 minutes

Difficulty: Easy

Ingredients:

- ✓ 500g (1 lb) champignon mushrooms, sliced
- ✓ 1 large onion, thinly sliced
- ✓ 2 tablespoons olive oil
- ✓ 1 teaspoon dried thyme
- ✓ Salt and pepper to taste
- ✓ Fresh parsley, chopped for garnish

Step-by-Step Preparation:

1. In a large bowl, toss the sliced champignons and onions with olive oil, dried thyme, salt, and pepper until evenly coated.

2. Preheat the air fryer to 360°F (180°C).

3. Spread the mushroom and onion mixture in the air fryer basket in a single layer.

4. Air fry for 15 minutes, shaking the basket halfway through, until the mushrooms are golden and the onions are tender.

5. Garnish with fresh parsley before serving.

Nutritional Facts: (Per serving)

- Calories: 110
- Protein: 6g
- Carbohydrates: 10g
- Fat: 6g
- Fiber: 2g
- Sodium: 15mg

Indulge in the earthy goodness of Roasted Sliced Champignons with Onions, a testament to how simple ingredients can transform into a dish full of deep flavors with the help of an air fryer. This recipe serves as a delicious side dish and stands out as a testament to healthy, high-protein eating, proving that nutritious meals can also be incredibly satisfying.

Recipe 37: Burger With Spinach and Vegetables

Dive into the vibrant world of Veggie Burgers with Spinach and Vegetables, a wholesome creation that brings the goodness of greens and the heartiness of vegetables into a delightful burger patty. Crafted with care for the air fryer, this high-protein vegetable recipe is a testament to healthy eating and a joy for the taste buds, proving that nourishing food can be both satisfying and delicious.

Servings: 4

Prepping Time: 20 minutes

Cook Time: 15 minutes

Difficulty: Medium

Ingredients:

- ✓ 1 cup cooked quinoa
- ✓ 1 can (15 oz) black beans, drained and rinsed
- ✓ 1 cup fresh spinach, finely chopped
- ✓ 1/2 cup carrots, grated
- ✓ 1/4 cup red onion, finely diced
- ✓ 2 cloves garlic, minced
- ✓ 1 teaspoon smoked paprika
- ✓ Salt and pepper to taste
- ✓ 2 tablespoons olive oil
- ✓ Whole wheat burger buns for serving
- ✓ Fresh lettuce and tomato slices for garnish

Step-by-Step Preparation:

1. In a large bowl, mash the black beans until mostly smooth.
2. Add cooked quinoa, chopped spinach, grated carrots, diced onion, minced garlic, smoked paprika, salt, and pepper to the mashed beans. Mix until well combined.
3. Form the mixture into 4 burger patties.
4. Preheat the air fryer to 375°F (190°C). Brush each patty with olive oil.
5. Air fry the patties for 15 minutes, flipping halfway through, until they are firm and golden.
6. Serve the veggie burgers with fresh lettuce and tomato slices on whole wheat buns.

Nutritional Facts: (Per serving)

- ❖ Calories: 315
- ❖ Protein: 14g
- ❖ Carbohydrates: 45g
- ❖ Fat: 10g
- ❖ Fiber: 10g
- ❖ Sodium: 200mg

Celebrate the joy of eating well with Veggie Burgers with Spinach and Vegetables, a dish that redefines the essence of fast food with its nutritional value and rich flavors. Perfect for any meal of the day, this recipe is a hearty, healthful way to enjoy the power of vegetables in a form everyone loves.

Recipe 38: Vegetarian Falafel With Tzatziki Sauce

Embark on a culinary journey to the Middle East with Fresh Vegetarian Falafel paired with creamy Tzatziki Sauce, a high-protein air fryer vegetable recipe that promises to delight. These crispy falafels, made from a blend of chickpeas, herbs, and spices, are perfectly complemented by the cool, tangy tzatziki, offering a nourishing and flavorful dish.

Servings: 4

Prepping Time: 20 minutes (plus soaking time for chickpeas)

Cook Time: 15 minutes

Difficulty: Medium

Ingredients:

- ✓ 1 cup dried chickpeas, soaked overnight
- ✓ 1/2 cup fresh parsley, chopped
- ✓ 1/4 cup fresh cilantro, chopped
- ✓ 3 cloves garlic, minced
- ✓ 1 small onion, chopped
- ✓ 1 teaspoon ground cumin
- ✓ 1 teaspoon ground coriander
- ✓ Salt and pepper to taste
- ✓ 2 tablespoons olive oil for brushing

For the Tzatziki Sauce:

- ✓ 1 cup Greek yogurt
- ✓ 1 cucumber, grated and drained
- ✓ 2 cloves garlic, minced
- ✓ 2 tablespoons fresh dill, chopped
- ✓ 1 tablespoon lemon juice
- ✓ Salt and pepper to taste

Step-by-Step Preparation:

1. Drain and rinse the soaked chickpeas. Combine them in a food processor with parsley, cilantro, garlic, onion, cumin, coriander, salt, and pepper. Process until well combined but still slightly coarse.
2. Form the mixture into small balls or patties.
3. Preheat the air fryer to 375°F (190°C). Brush the falafel with olive oil and place them in the air fryer basket.
4. Cook for 15 minutes, turning halfway through, until golden and crispy.
5. Mix Greek yogurt, grated cucumber, garlic, dill, lemon juice, salt, and pepper in a bowl for the tzatziki sauce. Chill until serving.
6. Serve falafels with tzatziki sauce on the side.

Nutritional Facts: (Per serving)

- ❖ Calories: 325
- ❖ Protein: 14g
- ❖ Carbohydrates: 45g
- ❖ Fat: 10g
- ❖ Fiber: 8g
- ❖ Sodium: 320mg

Enjoy the freshness and vibrancy of Vegetarian Falafel with Tzatziki Sauce, a recipe that brings together the best of Middle Eastern flavors in a health-conscious way. This dish celebrates taste and nutrition, making it a perfect addition to any meal where you desire something special yet utterly satisfying.

Recipe 39: Roman Fried Artichokes

Savor the taste of Rome with the classic Roman Fried Artichokes (Jewish Style), a dish where artichokes are transformed into a crispy, golden delicacy seasoned with flakes of sea salt. This high-protein, air fryer vegetable recipe brings a piece of Italian culinary tradition to your table, offering a modern twist on a beloved, healthy, and delicious classic.

Servings: 4

Prepping Time: 20 minutes

Cook Time: 20 minutes

Difficulty: Medium

Ingredients:

- ✓ 4 large artichokes
- ✓ 2 lemons, juiced
- ✓ 4 tablespoons olive oil
- ✓ Flakes of sea salt, to taste

- ✓ 2 cloves garlic, minced
- ✓ 1 teaspoon fresh parsley, chopped (for garnish)

Step-by-Step Preparation:

1. Prepare the artichokes by removing the outer leaves and trimming the tops and stems. Slice them in half and remove the fuzzy choke with a spoon.

2. Place artichoke halves in a bowl of water mixed with half of the lemon juice to prevent browning.

3. Drain the artichokes and pat dry. Toss them with olive oil, lemon juice, and minced garlic.

4. Preheat the air fryer to 390°F (200°C).

5. Arrange the artichokes in the air fryer basket, cut side down, and cook for 20 minutes or until golden and tender.

6. Season with sea salt flakes and garnish with chopped parsley before serving.

Nutritional Facts: (Per serving)

- ❖ Calories: 180
- ❖ Protein: 4g
- ❖ Carbohydrates: 15g

- ❖ Fat: 13g
- ❖ Fiber: 7g
- ❖ Sodium: 300mg

Experience the delight of Roman Fried Artichokes (Jewish Style) with Flakes of Sea Salt, a dish that captures the essence of Italian cuisine with the health benefits of air frying. This recipe celebrates the artichoke in its most flavorful form, perfect for a sophisticated side or a light main, proving that traditional dishes can be both nutritious and indulgent.

Recipe 40: Fried Zucchini and Tomato

Dive into the fresh, vibrant flavors of Fried Zucchini and Tomato, a vegetarian delight that marries the subtle sweetness of zucchini with the tangy richness of tomatoes. This high-protein air fryer vegetable recipe is a testament to the simplicity of ingredients, transforming them into a dish that's easy to prepare and packed with nutritional goodness, perfect for a light lunch or a side dish.

Servings: 4

Prepping Time: 10 minutes

Cook Time: 15 minutes

Difficulty: Easy

Ingredients:

- ✓ 2 large zucchinis, sliced
- ✓ 2 tomatoes, sliced
- ✓ 1 tablespoon olive oil
- ✓ 1 teaspoon dried oregano
- ✓ Salt and pepper to taste
- ✓ 2 tablespoons grated Parmesan cheese (optional)
- ✓ Fresh basil leaves for garnish

Step-by-Step Preparation:

1. Toss the sliced zucchini and tomatoes in a bowl with olive oil, dried oregano, salt, and pepper.

2. Preheat the air fryer to 380°F (190°C).

3. Arrange the vegetables in the air fryer basket in a single layer, ensuring they are not overlapping.

4. Cook for 15 minutes or until the vegetables are tender and slightly crispy around the edges.

5. If using, sprinkle the grated Parmesan cheese over the hot vegetables just before serving.

6. Garnish with fresh basil leaves.

Nutritional Facts: (Per serving)

- ❖ Calories: 76
- ❖ Protein: 3g
- ❖ Carbohydrates: 6g
- ❖ Fat: 5g
- ❖ Fiber: 2g
- ❖ Sodium: 75mg

Indulge in the comforting embrace of Fried Zucchini and Tomato, a dish that proves simplicity is the ultimate sophistication. With its light, healthful approach and a burst of flavors, this recipe is an ode to the beauty of vegetables, making it a perfect choice for anyone seeking a delicious and nutritious meal.

Chapter 05: Hearty Protein Snacks

Recipe 41: Roasted Peeled Peanuts

Embark on a crunchy journey with air fryer roasted, peeled peanuts, a high-protein snack effortlessly whipped in your kitchen. This snack is delicious and packs a nutritious punch, making it the perfect munch for any time of the day.

Servings: 4

Prepping Time: 5 minutes

Cook Time: 15 minutes

Difficulty: Easy

Ingredients:

- ✓ 2 cups of peeled peanuts
- ✓ 1 teaspoon of olive oil
- ✓ 1/2 teaspoon of salt (adjust to taste)
- ✓ Optional: 1/4 teaspoon of chili powder or your favorite spice for a kick

Step-by-Step Preparation:

1. Preheat your air fryer to 350°F (175°C).

2. Toss the peeled peanuts with olive oil and salt in a bowl until evenly coated. Add chili powder or your chosen spice if you like a bit of heat.

3. Spread the peanuts in a single layer in the air fryer basket.

4. Roast for about 15 minutes, shaking the basket halfway through, until golden and fragrant.

5. Allow to cool before serving, as they will crisp up further.

Nutritional Facts: (Per serving)

- ❖ Calories: 207
- ❖ Protein: 9.2g
- ❖ Fat: 18g
- ❖ Carbohydrates: 6.2g
- ❖ Fiber: 2.8g

Dive into the delightful crunch of homemade roasted peanuts straight from your air fryer. This simple, protein-rich snack satisfies your hunger pangs and brings a joyous crunch to your snack time. Perfect for sharing or enjoying solo, it's a guilt-free treat that will become a staple in your snacking repertoire.

Recipe 42: Air Fryer Gyoza

Discover the delightful crisp of air fryer gyoza, where traditional flavors meet modern convenience. This recipe for grilled pork and vegetable dumplings presents a high-protein snack that's satisfying and easy to prepare. These gyozas will become your new favorite way to enjoy a classic dish, perfect for a quick appetizer or a light meal.

Servings: 4

Prepping Time: 20 minutes

Cook Time: 10 minutes

Difficulty: Intermediate

Ingredients:

- ✓ 1/2 pound ground pork
- ✓ 1 cup finely chopped cabbage
- ✓ 2 green onions, finely chopped
- ✓ 2 garlic cloves, minced
- ✓ 1 tablespoon soy sauce
- ✓ 1 teaspoon sesame oil
- ✓ 1/2 teaspoon grated ginger
- ✓ Salt and pepper to taste
- ✓ 24 gyoza wrappers
- ✓ Water for sealing dumplings
- ✓ Olive oil spray for cooking

Step-by-Step Preparation:

1. Combine ground pork, cabbage, green onions, garlic, soy sauce, sesame oil, ginger, salt, and pepper in a large bowl. Mix well.
2. Place a spoonful of the filling in the center of each gyoza wrapper. Wet the edges with water and fold, pressing to seal.
3. Preheat the air fryer to 375°F (190°C). Lightly spray the gyoza with olive oil.
4. Arrange the gyozas in the air fryer basket, ensuring they don't touch. Cook in batches if necessary.
5. Cook for 10 minutes, flipping halfway through, until golden brown and crispy.
6. Serve hot with your favorite dipping sauce.

Nutritional Facts: (Per serving)

- ❖ Calories: 250
- ❖ Protein: 15g
- ❖ Fat: 10g
- ❖ Carbohydrates: 24g
- ❖ Fiber: 1g

Savor the irresistibly crispy exterior and juicy filling of these air fryer gyozas. A fusion of hearty pork and vegetables wrapped in a delicate dough, this dish brings a protein-packed twist to your snack time or meal prep. Quick, easy, and delicious, it's a culinary adventure that promises to delight your taste buds and fit seamlessly into your busy lifestyle.

Recipe 43: Crispy Garlic Bacon Bread

Indulge in the savory fusion of crispy garlic bacon bread, a delectable treat that combines the richness of butter, the aromatic allure of garlic, and the robust flavor of bacon; all encased in a golden, crispy bread. Made in the air fryer, this high-protein snack is mouthwatering and surprisingly easy to whip up, offering a perfect blend of flavor and crunch.

Servings: 4

Prepping Time: 10 minutes

Cook Time: 8 minutes

Difficulty: Easy

Ingredients:

- ✓ 4 slices of thick-cut bread
- ✓ 4 tablespoons unsalted butter, softened
- ✓ 2 cloves garlic, minced
- ✓ 4 strips of bacon, cooked and crumbled
- ✓ 1 tablespoon fresh parsley, chopped
- ✓ Salt to taste
- ✓ 1/4 cup grated Parmesan cheese (optional for added protein and flavor)

Step-by-Step Preparation:

1. Mix the softened butter with minced garlic, parsley, and a pinch of salt in a small bowl to create the garlic butter.
2. Spread the garlic butter evenly on one side of each bread slice.
3. Sprinkle the crumbled bacon (and Parmesan cheese if using) over the buttered side of each slice.
4. Place the bread slices in the air fryer basket, buttered side up.
5. Set the air fryer to 360°F (182°C) and cook for about 8 minutes until the bread is golden brown and crispy.
6. Serve immediately while hot and crispy.

Nutritional Facts: (Per serving)

- ❖ Calories: 330
- ❖ Protein: 12g
- ❖ Fat: 22g
- ❖ Carbohydrates: 22g
- ❖ Fiber: 1g

Experience the ultimate snack with crispy garlic bacon bread - a symphony of flavors that dance on your palate, marrying the crunch of bacon with the soft, buttery texture of perfectly toasted bread. This air fryer creation is a testament to the joy of simple ingredients transforming into a satisfying and delightfully easy snack. Perfect for any occasion, it's a high-protein treat that will leave you craving more.

Recipe 44: Tempeh or Tempe Goreng

Embark on a culinary journey with Air Fryer Tempeh, an iconic dish reimagined for the modern kitchen. This high-protein snack, Tempe Goreng in its traditional form, is given a healthy twist without sacrificing its beloved, savory crunch. Perfect for vegans and protein-seekers alike, this dish promises a delectable crunch with every bite, making it an ideal snack or side.

Servings: 4

Cook Time: 10 minutes

Prepping Time: 10 minutes

Difficulty: Easy

Ingredients:

- ✓ 8 oz (225g) tempeh, sliced
- ✓ 1 tablespoon soy sauce
- ✓ 1 tablespoon olive oil
- ✓ 1 teaspoon garlic powder
- ✓ 1/2 teaspoon smoked paprika
- ✓ Salt and pepper to taste

Step-by-Step Preparation:

1. Whisk together soy sauce, olive oil, garlic powder, smoked paprika, salt, and pepper in a small bowl.

2. Slice the tempeh into 1/4-inch thick pieces and place in a shallow dish.

3. Pour the marinade over the tempeh slices, ensuring each piece is evenly coated. Let it marinate for at least 5 minutes.

4. Preheat the air fryer to 375°F (190°C).

5. Arrange the tempeh slices in a single layer in the air fryer basket, ensuring they don't overlap.

6. Cook for 10 minutes, flipping halfway through, until the tempeh is golden brown and crispy on the edges.

7. Serve immediately, with dipping sauce if desired.

Nutritional Facts: **(Per serving)**

- ❖ Calories: 140
- ❖ Protein: 11g
- ❖ Fat: 9g
- ❖ Carbohydrates: 7g
- ❖ Fiber: 0g

Dive into the world of Air Fryer Tempeh, where traditional flavors meet modern health consciousness. This high-protein, vegan-friendly snack brings a crispy, savory delight to your table, perfect for any time of the day. Whether you're looking for a nutritious snack or a versatile side, this air-fried tempeh will surely impress with its ease and flavor.

Recipe 45: Tandoori Paneer Broccoli

Elevate your snacking game with Tandoori Paneer Broccoli, a vibrant and flavorful dish that pairs paneer's softness with broccoli's crunch. Marinated in a spiced yogurt mixture and perfectly cooked in an air fryer, this high-protein snack is a delicious twist on traditional Indian cuisine. Quick to prepare and packed with flavors, it's a healthy option for any time of day.

Servings: 4

Prepping Time: 15 minutes (plus marination time)

Cook Time: 15 minutes

Difficulty: Medium

Ingredients:

- ✓ 200g paneer (cottage cheese), cut into cubes
- ✓ 1 large broccoli head, cut into florets
- ✓ 1/2 cup plain yogurt
- ✓ 1 tablespoon tandoori masala
- ✓ 1 teaspoon turmeric powder
- ✓ 1 teaspoon garam masala
- ✓ 1 tablespoon lemon juice
- ✓ Salt to taste
- ✓ 1 tablespoon olive oil

Step-by-Step Preparation:

1. Mix yogurt, tandoori masala, turmeric powder, garam masala, lemon juice, and salt in a large bowl to create the marinade.
2. Add paneer cubes and broccoli florets to the bowl, gently tossing to ensure they are fully coated with the marinade. Cover and refrigerate for at least 30 minutes.
3. Preheat the air fryer to 360°F (182°C).
4. Lightly brush the air fryer basket with olive oil. Arrange the marinated paneer and broccoli in a single layer, ensuring they are not overcrowded.
5. Air fry for 15 minutes, turning halfway through, until the paneer is golden and broccoli is tender.
6. Serve immediately, garnished with a squeeze of lemon or a sprinkle of chaat masala for an extra flavor boost.

Nutritional Facts: (Per serving)

- ❖ Calories: 180
- ❖ Protein: 12g
- ❖ Fat: 10g
- ❖ Carbohydrates: 9g
- ❖ Fiber: 3g

Tandoori Paneer Broccoli offers a delightful way to enjoy your greens and proteins in one go. This dish caters to your taste buds with its spicy and tangy flavors and to your body's nutritional needs. Ideal for those seeking a healthy yet flavorful snack, it promises a guilt-free indulgence that can be enjoyed at any time, adding a burst of color and nutrients to your day.

Recipe 46: Fried Fish Cake

Dive into the flavors of Thailand with Tod Mun Pla Krai, a beloved snack that combines the zest of minced seafish with the fiery punch of roasted chili curry. This version brings a modern twist to the classic using an air fryer, offering a healthier alternative without compromising taste. High in protein and full of flavor, these fish cakes are a perfect snack for any occasion.

Servings: 4

Prepping Time: 20 minutes

Cook Time: 15 minutes

Difficulty: Medium

Ingredients:

- ✓ 1 pound minced sea fish (such as cod or tilapia)
- ✓ 2 tablespoons roasted chili curry paste
- ✓ 1 egg, beaten
- ✓ 2 tablespoons finely chopped green beans

- ✓ 1 teaspoon sugar
- ✓ 1 tablespoon fish sauce
- ✓ 1/4 cup finely sliced kaffir lime leaves
- ✓ Fresh cilantro for garnish

Step-by-Step Preparation:

1. Mix the minced fish with roasted chili curry paste in a large bowl until well combined.
2. Add the beaten egg, chopped green beans, sugar, fish sauce, and sliced kaffir lime leaves to the fish mixture. Stir until the mixture becomes sticky and homogenous.
3. Preheat the air fryer to 350°F (177°C).
4. Form the fish mixture into small patties about 2 inches in diameter.
5. Place the fish cakes in the air fryer basket, ensuring they do not touch. You may need to cook them in batches, depending on the size of your air fryer.
6. Cook for 15 minutes, flipping halfway through, until the fish cakes are golden brown and cooked.
7. Serve hot, garnished with fresh cilantro.

Nutritional Facts: (Per serving)

- ❖ Calories: 195
- ❖ Protein: 23g
- ❖ Fat: 5g

- ❖ Carbohydrates: 10g
- ❖ Fiber: 1g

Tod Mun Pla Krai offers a delightful way to enjoy the essence of Thai cuisine with a healthy twist. These air-fried fish cakes are easy on the calories and pack a protein punch, making them an excellent snack for health-conscious foodies and adventurous eaters alike. Perfect for dipping, sharing, or enjoying solo, this dish promises a deliciously satisfying experience with every bite.

Recipe 47: Churros With Chocolate Sauce

Indulge in a classic Spanish dessert with a twist: Air Fryer Churros with Chocolate Sauce. This high-protein version offers a healthier alternative to the traditionally deep-fried treat, allowing you to enjoy the same deliciously doughy texture and sweet, crispy exterior without the guilt. Paired with a rich chocolate sauce, these churros make the perfect snack or dessert for any occasion.

Servings: 4

Prepping Time: 15 minutes

Cook Time: 10 minutes

Difficulty: Medium

Ingredients:

- ✓ 1 cup water
- ✓ 1/3 cup unsalted butter
- ✓ 2 tablespoons sugar
- ✓ 1/4 teaspoon salt
- ✓ 1 cup all-purpose flour
- ✓ 3 large eggs
- ✓ 1 teaspoon vanilla extract
- ✓ Protein powder (optional to increase protein content)
- ✓ Cinnamon sugar for coating
- ✓ **For the Chocolate Sauce:**
- ✓ 1/2 cup heavy cream
- ✓ 4 ounces dark chocolate, chopped
- ✓ 1 tablespoon sugar

Step-by-Step Preparation:

1. Combine water, butter, sugar, and salt in a saucepan over medium heat. Bring to a boil, remove from heat, and stir in the flour until well combined.
2. Add eggs and vanilla extract, mixing until a smooth dough forms. If desired, incorporate protein powder at this stage.
3. Transfer the dough to a piping bag fitted with a large star nozzle.
4. Preheat the air fryer to 350°F (180°C). Pipe the dough into 6-inch lengths, cutting with scissors, onto the air fryer basket.
5. Cook for 10 minutes or until golden brown. Roll the warm churros in cinnamon sugar.
6. **For the Chocolate Sauce:**
7. Heat the cream in a small saucepan until it just begins to simmer. Remove from heat and stir in the chocolate and sugar until smooth.
8. Serve the churros with the warm chocolate sauce for dipping.

Nutritional Facts: (Per serving)

- ❖ Calories: 300
- ❖ Protein: 5g
- ❖ Fat: 18g
- ❖ Carbohydrates: 27g
- ❖ Fiber: 1g

Embrace the joy of cooking with these Air Fryer Churros and homemade Chocolate Sauce, a recipe that combines the comfort of warm, sweet dough with the indulgence of dark chocolate. Whether you're looking for a delightful finish to your meal or a special snack to brighten your day, these high-protein churros offer a healthier way to satisfy your cravings.

Recipe 48: Yam Fries Bake by Air Fryer

Dive into the sweet, earthy flavors of Yam Fries, a healthier twist on a beloved snack. Baked to perfection in an air fryer, these yam fries offer a crispy exterior and a soft, tender interior. This high-protein version is seasoned with spices that elevate the natural sweetness of the yams, making it an irresistible, guilt-free treat for any time of the day.

Servings: 4

Prepping Time: 10 minutes

Cook Time: 15 minutes

Difficulty: Easy

Ingredients:

- ✓ 2 large yams, peeled and cut into fries
- ✓ 1 tablespoon olive oil
- ✓ 1 teaspoon paprika
- ✓ 1/2 teaspoon garlic powder
- ✓ 1/2 teaspoon onion powder
- ✓ Salt and pepper to taste
- ✓ Optional: sprinkle of protein powder for an extra protein boost

Step-by-Step Preparation:

1. Preheat the air fryer to 400°F (200°C).
2. In a large bowl, toss the yam fries with olive oil, paprika, garlic powder, onion powder, salt, pepper, and optional protein powder until evenly coated.
3. Arrange the fries in a single layer in the air fryer basket, ensuring they don't overlap for even cooking. You may need to work in batches.
4. Air fry for about 15 minutes, flipping halfway through or until the fries are crispy and golden brown.
5. Serve immediately with your choice of dipping sauce or as a standalone snack.

Nutritional Facts: (Per serving)

- ❖ Calories: 140
- ❖ Protein: 2g (more with protein powder)
- ❖ Fat: 3.5g
- ❖ Carbohydrates: 26g
- ❖ Fiber: 4g

Yam Fries baked in an air fryer are a delightful way to enjoy a classic snack with a nutritious twist. Whether seeking a healthy side dish or a satisfying snack, these crispy, high-protein yam fries will surely please your palate and support your dietary goals. They're a testament to the joy of simple, wholesome ingredients quickly prepared and packed with flavor.

Recipe 49: Puff Pastry Air Fryer Pigs

Discover the delight of making Puff Pastry Air Fryer Pigs, a crispy, protein-packed snack perfect for any time of the day. Enjoy the convenience of your air fryer with this simple yet satisfying recipe.

Servings: 4

Prepping Time: 15 minutes

Cook Time: 15 minutes

Difficulty: Easy

Ingredients:

- ✓ 1 sheet of puff pastry, thawed
- ✓ 8 turkey sausages
- ✓ 1 egg, beaten (for egg wash)
- ✓ 1 tsp of sesame seeds (optional, for garnish)
- ✓ Mustard or ketchup for serving

Step-by-Step Preparation:

1. Preheat your air fryer to 375°F (190°C).

2. Cut the puff pastry into strips about 1 inch wide.

3. Wrap each sausage in a pastry strip, sealing the edges with water.

4. Brush the top of each pastry-wrapped sausage with the beaten egg and sprinkle with sesame seeds if using.

5. Place in the air fryer basket, ensuring they're not touching, and cook for 15 minutes or until golden and puffed.

6. Serve immediately with mustard or ketchup for dipping.

Nutritional Facts: (Per serving)

- ❖ Calories: 320
- ❖ Protein: 14g
- ❖ Fat: 22g
- ❖ Carbohydrates: 18g
- ❖ Sodium: 670mg

Embrace the joy of homemade snacks with these Puff Pastry Air Fryer Pigs. They're a breeze to prepare and a delicious way to include more protein in your snacks. These crispy delights will become a new favorite, perfect for parties or a family treat.

Recipe 50: Grilled Salmon Belly With Salt

Unveil the savory world of Grilled Salmon Belly with Salt, a high-protein snack that combines simplicity with the sumptuous richness of salmon. This air fryer recipe transforms salmon belly into a crisp, golden delicacy with just the right touch of seasoning.

Servings: 2

Cook Time: 8 minutes

Prepping Time: 10 minutes

Difficulty: Easy

Ingredients:

- ✓ 2 salmon belly strips, about 150g each
- ✓ 1 tbsp olive oil
- ✓ Coarse sea salt, to taste
- ✓ Freshly ground black pepper, to taste
- ✓ Lemon wedges for serving

Step-by-Step Preparation:

1. Preheat the air fryer to 400°F (200°C).
2. Pat the salmon belly strips dry with paper towels.
3. Rub each strip with olive oil and season generously with coarse sea salt and black pepper.
4. Place the salmon belly strips in the air fryer basket, skin-side down, and cook for 8 minutes until the skin is crispy and the flesh is tender and flaky.
5. Serve immediately with lemon wedges on the side.

Nutritional Facts: (Per serving)

- ❖ Calories: 310
- ❖ Protein: 23g
- ❖ Fat: 23g
- ❖ Carbohydrates: 0g
- ❖ Sodium: 590mg

Delight in the elegant simplicity of Grilled Salmon Belly with Salt, a dish that promises to elevate your snack time with its perfect blend of flavors and textures. This air fryer masterpiece is a testament to the beauty of minimalistic cooking, offering a healthy, protein-rich treat that's as nutritious as it is delicious.

Conclusion

As we wrap up your journey through the "Crisp High Protein Air Fryer Power Meals Cookbook," we hope that these pages have provided you with delicious recipes and inspired you to embrace a healthier, protein-rich diet using the convenience of your air fryer. Bella Bistro has crafted each recipe passionately for nutrition and flavor, ensuring that each dish supports your health and satisfies your taste buds.

Throughout the five chapters—Chicken, Meat, Fish & Seafood, Vegetables, and Snacks—you've been introduced to 50 innovative recipes, each one designed to make high-protein eating effortless and enjoyable. From succulent chicken dishes and robust meat options to fresh seafood creations and hearty vegetable sides, every recipe has been tailored to add nutritional value and culinary delight to your daily meals.

Key Takeaways from Your Experience:

- **Diverse and Nutritious Recipes:** With 50 unique, high-protein dishes, this cookbook has expanded your culinary horizons, providing new ways to enjoy healthy eating at every meal.

- **Authentic and Original Cooking:** Each recipe, developed by Bella Bistro, is an authentic creation, promising originality and freshness in your cooking.

- **High-Quality Visuals and Print:** The vibrant, original photos and standard color printing enhance your experience, making the recipes as appealing visually as they are nutritionally.

- **Simplicity in Instructions:** The clear, easy-to-follow guidelines have hopefully made cooking less daunting, allowing you to achieve perfect results effortlessly.

- **Perfectly Tested Flavors:** Rigorous testing has ensured that each dish meets high protein standards and excels in flavor, making healthy eating a pleasure rather than a chore.

- **Error-Free Content:** The attention to detail in editing guarantees a smooth reading experience, letting you focus entirely on enjoying and preparing your meals.

Thank you for choosing this cookbook as your companion on a healthier lifestyle. Continue to use these recipes as your go-to resource for high-protein cooking with your air fryer. Bella Bistro is excited to be part of your kitchen adventures and looks forward to continuing this journey with you, one flavorful, protein-packed meal at a time. Happy cooking!

Made in United States
Cleveland, OH
19 December 2024

12385543R00059